DANIEL

Hostage in Babylon

DANIEL

Hostage in Babylon

Kendall K. Down

Typeset using "Ovation", a DeskTop Publishing program
for the Archimedes range of computers
using 10 pt Paladin, a Palatino equivalent.
The printing plates were reproduced from originals
printed using a Apple LaserWriter II

ISBN 0-904748-67-7

Printed by

The Stanborough Press Limited

Alma Park, Grantham, Lincolnshire, NG31 9SL

Table of Contents

DANIEL

Introduction

I have long been fascinated by the period spanned by the life of the Biblical prophet Daniel. Possibly my interest is due to the similarities between Daniel's time and our own.

The twentieth century has seen the fall of the British Empire, an empire which at the beginning of the century seemed invincible. We have seen continual trouble in the Middle East, where Egypt in particular, under Gamel Abdul Nasser, has tried to bring the surrounding nations under its sway. More recently we see Saddam Hussein in Iraq, a man who deliberately draws parallels between himself and Nebuchadnezzar, making the same bid for domination.

At the same time we also see God's people - the Christian church - under increasing pressure from the heathen forces around it. In this latter part of the twentieth century the New Age movement, with its mixture of heathen philosophy and occult mysticism, seems to be winning the battle for the minds and souls of men while the God of the Christians is strangely silent.

To the Jews of Daniel's day also it must have seemed that God was strangely silent. Jerusalem, abandoned to the vengeful Chaldeans; the gods of Babylon in the ascendant and the temple of Jehovah in ruins. Yet through the prophet God spoke a message of hope, a message concerning a kingdom which would never pass away.

This message was not given to the Jews alone. Its meaning and significance was hidden by symbols and time-scales until the "time of the end". Only then would the wise be able to understand the vision.

I believe that we are living in that "time of the end" and therefore the Book of Daniel contains a vitally important message for us. Despite the discouraging circumstances that confront us we can have the assurance that God is in control of history. God's plans and purposes know no delay, man cannot hinder them nor evil vanquish them. One day, very soon now, "Michael will arise" and God's people will be delivered.

I have travelled extensively in the Middle East and have drawn upon personal knowledge both of the people and the places to flesh out the historical background to the Book of Daniel. If I have made this important book of the Bible a little more interesting to you or even a little more understandable, then I shall be well pleased.

The Author.

DANIEL

Chapter 1

Soon after he came to the throne of Babylon Nabopolassar revolted against his Assyrian overlords. Each summer thereafter the Chaldean armies took the field, fighting for their independence against the forces of the Assyrian empire.

Despite near defeat in 616 BC, Nabopolassar attempted to capture Asshur the following year. Again he failed. The Babylonians alone could not hope to defeat Assyria. In the year 612 BC therefore, he made a treaty with Cyraxes, king of the Medes, a tribe of fierce hill-men who were also fighting the Assyrians.

The combined armies attacked Nineveh and all through the hot summer months they skirmished unsuccessfully beneath its mighty walls. Then fate took a hand. The Tigris began to rise, its brown water surging against the river bank, tearing great chunks of earth away. Nothing man-made could withstand the pressure. With a tremendous roar the city's river wall collapsed and was swept away.

Almost immediately the flood began to subside, leaving a great hole in the city's defences. The Median warriors poured through the breach and Sin-Shar-Ishkun, the last king of Nineveh, died in the flames of his palace.

"The chariots storm through the streets, rushing back and forth through the squares. They look like flaming torches; they dart about like lightning. He summons his picked troops, yet they stumble on their way. They dash to the city wall; the protective shield is put in place. The river gates are thrown open and the palace collapses. . . . Charging cavalry, flashing

swords and glittering spears! Many casualties, piles of dead, bodies without number, people stumbling over the corpses." Nahum 2:4-6; 3:3

The Assyrian crown prince Assur-Uballit escaped the sack of Nineveh and fled to Haran where he tried to re-group his forces. Meanwhile the small nations of Palestine looked about apprehensively to see who would replace the Assyrians as dominant power.

After looting Nineveh the Medes withdrew to their isolated mountain fastnesses but the Babylonians began a series of aggressive summer campaigns designed to annihilate the last remnants of the hated Assyrian empire and ensure their own position in the Middle East.

There was, however, another contender as successor to the Assyrians. The Egyptians were no more willing to endure a Babylonian yoke than they had been to accept the Assyrian one. They decided that weak Assyria made a more comfortable neighbour than strong Babylon. In the spring of 609 BC Pharaoh Necho led his army northwards to support Assur-Uballit against Nabopolassar.[1]

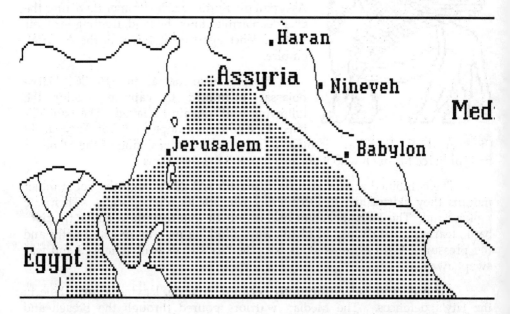

Since the days of Hezekiah Judah had been friendly towards Babylon,[2] so King Josiah determined to help the Babylonians by opposing the Egyptian advance. For thousands of years Palestinian generals had chosen to attack the Egyptian army in the pass near Megiddo.[3] Here the road north left the narrowing coastal plain and crossed the Carmel range to the plain of Jezreel.

Hemmed in by rugged hills, the formidable chariotry of Egypt could not deploy, thus giving Judah's infantry a better chance.

As Josiah led his army out of Jerusalem, three men watched it with very different emotions. The middle-aged prophet Jeremiah must have felt a lively apprehension at seeing the king who shared his religious ideals risking his life for political gain. Outside the temple Ezekiel, the 13 year old son of a priest, may have been busy helping his father collect offerings and register vows from soldiers anxious to ensure a safe return. Daniel, who would have been about the same age, may well have been cajoling his high-born father to allow him to go on the expedition too.

We do not know the reason for what happened next. Perhaps the Judeans arrived too late at the pass. Perhaps the Egyptians were just too strong. The Egyptians forced their way down onto the plain of Jezreel. On the flat fields below Megiddo the chariots were able to charge and wheel and charge again. The army of Judah was destroyed; King Josiah himself was among the slain.[4]

The surviving nobles chose one of Josiah's sons and crowned him but Judah was in no state to withstand the Egyptians when Necho returned in vengeful mood. His first action was to depose Jehoahaz, who may also have been pro-Babylonian.[5] In his place Necho chose another of Josiah's sons - Eliakim and changed his name to Jehoiakim, fined the country heavily for its former defiance and then departed, taking the unfortunate Jehoahaz with him to Egypt, where he spent the rest of his life in captivity.

Three years passed, with relative peace in Palestine. Each year the Egyptian army marched north to Haran where the Babylonians were trying to force their way across the Euphrates. Each year the campaign closed in stalemate, with neither side gaining a decisive advantage.

In 605 BC the aging Nabopolassar was too ill to command his army in the field. He appointed his son, Nebuchadnezzar, to lead in his place. It was a fortunate decision. With brilliant generalship Nebuchadnezzar smashed the Egyptian army and pursued the fleeing remnants down through Palestine, accepting the surrender of the smaller states on the way. Among the cities which opened their gates was the city of Jerusalem.

"In the third year of the reign of Jehoiakim king of Judah, Nebuchadnezzar king of Babylon came to Jerusalem and besieged it." Daniel 1:1

Nebuchadnezzar only stayed long enough to loot some of the temple treasures, then continued on towards the Egyptian border. It seemed certain that Egypt would be invaded, but the campaign ended abruptly. A dispatch rider, who had followed the army around the Fertile Crescent, galloped into the Babylonian camp with a message: Nabopolassar was dead and a party of loyal noblemen was holding the throne for Prince Nebuchadnezzar, but he must hurry home to ensure his succession.

Nebuchadnezzar appointed his chief eunuch as army commander, for eunuchs were supposed to be devoid of ambition. There was no time to set governors and garrisons in the conquered territories so Ashpenaz was instructed to take hostages and lead the army home while Nebuchadnezzar and a few companions galloped straight across the desert to Babylon - five hundred miles of waterless desolation. Centuries later historians still spoke of the feat with awe and admiration.

"Then the king ordered Ashpenaz, chief of his court officials, to bring in some of the Israelites from the royal family and the nobility - young men without any physical defect, handsome, showing aptitude for every kind of learning, well informed, quick to understand and qualified to serve in the king's palace. He was to teach them the language and literature of the Babylonians." Daniel 1:3, 4

Taking hostages was a well established ritual in Middle Eastern diplomatic arrangements. The victors demanded the eldest sons and potential heirs while defeated rulers tried to substitute younger sons and the children of less favoured wives. It is for this reason that we can be sure the young men eventually selected belonged to the nobility of Judah and possibly even the royal household.

"Among these were some from Judah: Daniel, Hananiah, Mishael and Azariah. The chief official gave them new names: to Daniel, the name Belteshazzar; to Hananiah, Shadrach; to Mishael, Meshach; and to Azariah, Abednego." Daniel 1:6, 7

Two of the four young men bore Hebrew names that included the sacred name of God - "Jah", while the names of the other two simply referred to God - "El". Not only did the Babylonians find these names outlandish and hard to pronounce, but they also wished to change the allegiance of the captives to the gods and kings of Babylon. The names given to them included references to the Babylonian gods Bel and Nego (or Nabu).

The army returned home by the route through Haran and along the Fertile Crescent. Hostages from all the conquered countries marched with the army, treated no doubt with rough courtesy and consideration, but strictly guarded. Their parents' loyalty to Babylon depended upon their presence in Babylonian hands.

Equally, the hostages' lives depended upon the continued loyalty of their parents. They must have known that such loyalty was fickle, that sooner or later the Egyptians would return to force a change in allegiance and then their lives would be forfeit to Chaldean anger. In such an eventuality their only hope lay in having ingratiated themselves with the Babylonians to such an extent that their lives would be spared. Yet it was in these circumstances that Daniel and his friends reached a momentous decision.

"But Daniel resolved not to defile himself with the royal food and wine." Daniel 1:8

Not only did the Babylonians eat unclean meats as defined in the eleventh chapter of Leviticus, but even the clean animals were slaughtered in the temples and thus dedicated to the heathen gods. In the same way wine was also dedicated to the gods of Babylon and was therefore unclean in Jewish eyes.

Daniel and his friends realised that their God was God of all the world, not just a local deity whose influence extended no further than the boundaries of a city state. They determined to continue to serve the God of heaven and the first requirement of such service was ritual purity. At the risk of incurring royal displeasure, Daniel approached the official in charge of the hostages.

"He asked the chief official for permission not to defile himself in this way. Now God had caused the official to show favour and sympathy to Daniel, but the official told Daniel, 'I am afraid of my lord the king, who has assigned your food and drink.'" Daniel 1:8-10

In the corrupt courts of the Middle East it was a well known perk for officials to substitute food of lesser quality and sell the better for their own profit. Like all new rulers, Nebuchadnezzar was determined to stamp out such practices and the penalty for embezzlement was death.

The official feared that on the restricted diet Daniel proposed the health of all four would suffer, enquiries would be made and the fact that they were not eating the same food as the rest of the hostages would be discovered. The obvious danger was that the true explanation would be disbelieved and the official would lose his head on a charge of corruption.

When the chief eunuch refused his request Daniel next approached the guard or tutor appointed to oversee their training. His request this time was more modest:

"'Please test your servants for ten days: give us nothing but vegetables to eat and water to drink. Then compare our appearance with that of the young men who eat the royal food and treat your servants in accordance with what you see.' So he agreed to this and tested them for ten days. At the end of the ten days they looked healthier and better nourished than any of the young men who ate the royal food." Daniel 1:12-15

For the preceding couple of months, as the army marched the dreary miles around the Fertile Crescent, the captives had subsisted on sparse army rations. That and the plentiful exercise of tramping the day's journey had kept them healthy. Suddenly they were at ease in Babylon, being fed on the rich, greasy, highly spiced dishes of a king, washed down with plenty of the very best wines.

No wonder that at the end of ten days Daniel and his companions looked healthier than any of the other hostages. Hang-overs, dysentery and upset stomachs were probably the least that those young men were suffering, and the contrast with the clear-eyed health of the four Jewish captives was startling. The tutor had no hesitation in allowing them to continue their vegetarian diet.

Although the Jewish religion did not call for vegetarianism, the first chapter of the book of Genesis makes it plain that man's original diet was purely vegetarian. In fact, man was only granted permission to eat meat after the flood, when all green things had been destroyed.

Isaiah's promise that one day, "The wolf will live with the lamb, . . . and a little child will lead them."[6] obviously predicts that the diet of Eden Restored will also be vegetarian.

Today, when the good things of the earth are freely available on the shelves of our supermarkets, there can be no doubt that the vegetarian diet is the best. Those who follow the example of Daniel and his friends and live on vegetables and water can expect to reap rewards of health, stamina and long life.

Seventh-day Adventists have long been largely vegetarian and, following Paul's statement that "your body is the temple of the Holy Ghost"[7], have adopted a drug-free life-style, abstaining from tobacco, alcohol and even tea and coffee. As a result repeated scientific studies have shown that Seventh-day Adventists enjoy better health and live significantly longer than the general population.

Increasingly, however, the difference between the health and longevity of Seventh-day Adventists and other people is being eroded as the world at large becomes more health conscious. More and more people are adopting the Seventh-day Adventist way of life, not because they adhere to a particular religion, but because they recognise the advantages of such a life-style.

The tragedy is that so many Christians, misled by a false theology that regards God's laws as a burden imposed by an inscrutable Providence upon the Jews, have failed to benefit from the advice of our loving Father. The dirt, disease and plagues of the Middle Ages could never have existed had the laws of Leviticus been strictly kept. Even today, as Seventh-day Adventists have shown, modern man can benefit by following the wise counsel of God, whether or not he understands God's reasons for the counsel.

In adition to the natural results of a healthy diet, God honoured the faithfulness and courage of these young men.

"To these four young men God gave knowledge and understanding of all kinds of literature and learning. . . . In every matter of wisdom and understanding about which the king questioned them, he found them ten times better than all the magicians and enchanters in his whole kingdom." Daniel 1:17, 20

A brain kept clear by abstension from alcohol and other drugs, by regular habits and by a healthy diet, was the reward that Daniel and his friends reaped. It is the reward open to all who today will follow their example in honouring God by keeping their bodies healthy.

"Do you not know that your body is a temple of the Holy Spirit, Who is in you, Whom you have received from God?. . . So whether you eat or drink or whatever you do, do it all for the glory of God." 1 Corinthians 6:19; 10:31

---

1. 2 Kings 23:29

2. 2 Kings 20:12

3. The Egptian army's strength lay in its terrible chariots which, like modern tanks, required room for manouvre. The wide deserts of Libya, Nubia and Sinai and the coastal plain of southern Palestine provided sufficient space for them to deploy effectively. However as the army marched northwards into Canaan the coastal plain narrowed till, where the Carmel range meets the sea there was nothing more than a track between cliff and water. As far back as Egyptian records go, their armies always detoured across the Carmel range and down onto the wide plain of Jezreel.

4. 2 Chronicles 35:25

5. Jehoiakim was the elder brother by two years, but the people for some reason made Jehoahaz king instead of his brother. He was obviously displeasing to Necho, so cannot have been pro-Egyptian. It is interesting to note that later on, when Nebuchadnezzar replaced Jehoiakim, he chose one of Jehoahaz' brothers - Zedekiah.

6. Isaiah 11:6-9

7. 1 Corinthians 6:19

DANIEL

Chapter 2

For three years Daniel, his three friends and the other hostages studied the learning of Babylon. They completed their course during the official second year of Nebuchadnezzar's reign. One morning, not long after their graduation, the king woke early with a vague feeling that something significant had occurred during the night.

"In the second year of his reign[1], Nebuchadnezzar had dreams; his mind was troubled and he could not sleep. So the king summoned the magicians, enchanters, sorcerers and astrologers to tell him what he had dreamed." Daniel 2:1, 2

According to the Chaldean belief, dreams were the means by which the gods communicated with man. The common people were given messages relating to common and personal affairs. The king, as divinely appointed head of the nation and semi-divine in his own right, received messages that affected the whole nation. It was obviously important for the nation that such messages should be understood.

To assist in the process of interpreting dreams, the temples contained libraries of clay tablets that set out dreams and their interp-

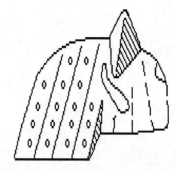

Babylonian model of a liver used for divination.

retations. These contained detailed notes similar to: "If a man dream of buried money - interpretation: sorrow will befall him."

Other methods of discovering the will of the gods included divination by such natural events as the flight of birds or the fall of a bundle of arrows, augury by examination of the liver of a sacrificial animal, and astrology. Clay models of livers, with the significant features labelled, have been found by archaeologists among the ruins of Babylon.

It was only natural therefore, when Nebuchadnezzar realised that the source of his disquiet was a portentious dream, that he should send for the specialists - the priests and sorcerers who claimed the ability to interpret the divine will.

"When they came in and stood before the king, he said to them, 'I have had a dream that troubles me and I want to know what it means.' Then the astrologers answered the king in Aramaic[2], 'O king, live for ever! Tell your servants the dream and we will interpret it.'" Daniel 2:4

Nebuchadnezzar claimed that he had forgotten the dream, and demanded that the priests should not only interpret the dream, but tell it as well. His claim of forgetfulness may of course be true, but we must not overlook the fact that Nebuchadnezzar was a young and brilliant man. Like most young rulers he looked for a way of breaking the entrenched power of any potential opposition, which in Babylon included the priesthood. He may also have been testing the truth of priestly claims.

"'You have conspired to tell me misleading and wicked things, hoping the situation will change. So then, tell me the dream, and I will know that you can interpret it for me.'" Daniel 2:9

According to the theology of Babylonian religion, the gods actually lived among mankind. The great temple tower, E-temen-anki, built in seven stages to a height of 300 feet, was surmounted by a small room richly adorned with tons of gold. The great god Marduk was supposed to sleep in this room - and a virgin was supplied each night for the god's convenience.

In theory it would be simple for the priests to send a message with the virgin, asking the god to repeat the dream or interpret it directly to the king. In practice of course, the priests knew very well that the room on top of the ziggurat remained empty; hence their desperation when confronted with the king's demand.

"The astrologers answered the king, 'There is not a man on earth who can do what the king asks! No king, however great and mighty, has ever asked such a thing of any magician or enchanter or astrologer. What the king asks is too difficult. No-one can reveal it to the king except the gods, and they do not live among men.'" Daniel 2:10, 11

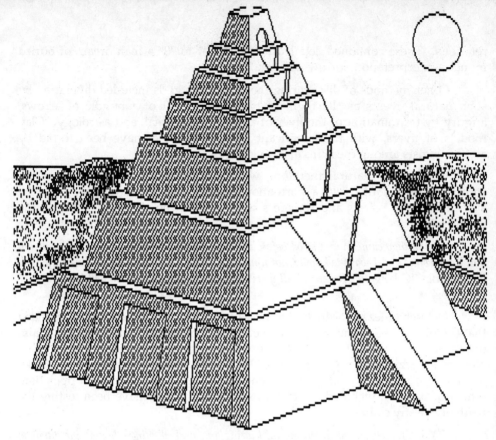

A ziggurat or temple tower of Mesopotamia

Buried deep beneath layers of myth and legend, the Babylonians possessed the concept of yet higher gods than the ones they worshipped. These gods were too remote and too mighty to concern themselves with the affairs of men, yet it was to this level that the Chaldeans appealed as an excuse for their failure to fulfil the king's request.

With a fine show of fury, Nebuchadnezzar ordered the immediate execution of the entire order of priests and magicians. As junior members of that order, Daniel and his friends had not been called upon to appear before the king but they were not exempt from his decree. The sacred college was surrounded by loyal troops and the inmates were led out to the place of execution.

Although they dared not disobey the king, the soldiers must have felt a superstitious fear as they prepared for this act of sacrilege. It is to their credit that they were neither hardened nor brutal and when Daniel enquired the reason for his impending death, he was courteously answered.

"When Arioch, the commander of the king's guard, had gone out to put to death the wise men of Babylon, Daniel spoke to him with wisdom and tact. He asked the king's officer, 'Why did the king issue such a harsh decree?' Arioch then explained the matter to Daniel. At this Daniel went in to the king and asked for time, so that he might interpret the dream for him." Daniel 2:14-16

It is unlikely that Daniel actually appeared before Nebuchadnezzar, or that he would have been given the freedom to do so. Probably his request was passed up the chain of command through officials and secretaries, one of whom may have been responsible for suggesting to the king that a twenty-four hour delay would do no harm and would expose the deceptions of the priests more clearly.

Daniel, and probably the other priests and wise men, returned to the temple precincts under a form of house arrest. There he explained the situation to his friends mystified by their sudden arrest and unexpected reprieve..

"He urged them to plead for mercy from the God of heaven concerning this mystery, so that he and his friends might not be executed with the rest of the wise men of Babylon." Daniel 2:18

Then, amazingly, they went to sleep! With a clear conscience even the prospect of death on the morrow was not enough to keep them awake. Added to this was their trust in the God of heaven that all would happen according to His will and in that they were perfectly content.

Their trust was not misplaced. During the night Daniel was given a dream and an interpretation which were still vivid in his mind when he awoke. His first action was to thank God for answering his prayer, even though he had not yet appeared before Nebuchadnezzar to receive confirmation that the two dreams were the same.

" 'I thank and praise You, O God of my fathers: You have given me wisdom and power, You have made known to me what we asked of You, You have made known to us the dream of the king.' " Daniel 2:23

After thanking God, Daniel went out and presented himself to Arioch. This time Arioch accompanied him as he was led directly into the presence of Nebuchadnezzar. With typical Eastern opportunism Arioch declared:

" 'I have found a man among the exiles from Judah who can tell the king what his dream means.' " Daniel 2:23

As if Arioch, the king's faithful servant, had spent the intervening night in sleepless search for someone to fulfil his royal master's desire! Nebuchadnezzar looked at the young student who stood confidently before him.

"'Are you able to tell me what I saw in my dream and interpret it?'" Daniel 2:26

With due reverence Daniel disclaimed any special power or wisdom of his own. He did not wish to claim anything for himself, instead he pointed the heathen king towards the source of all wisdom.

"'No wise man, enchanter, magician or deviner can explain to the king the mystery he has asked about, but there is a God in heaven who reveals mysteries. He has shown King Nebuchadnezzar what will happen in days to come.'" Daniel 2:27, 28

Many people today turn to enchanters and magicians in order to discover secret wisdom or the hidden mysteries of the future. They seek to tap into mysterious forces of nature or a supposed higher plane of consciousness. Sometimes these occult practices are even masked under a guise of Christianity, but the God of the Bible will have nothing to do with them.

"Let no-one be found among you who practises divination or sorcery, interprets omens, engages in witchcraft, or casts spells, or who is a medium or spiritist or who consults the dead. Anyone who does these things is detestable to the Lord." Deuteronomy 18:10-12

Daniel's triumphant words were "There is a God in heaven!" Those who trust in occult practitioners will inevitably be brought to darkness and confusion. Those who trust in God will find, as Daniel found, light and peace.

"If any of you lacks wisdom, he should ask God, who gives generously to all . . . , and it will be given to him." James 1:5

Daniel continued by explaining to the king the purpose of his dream, the reason why he had been visited by God.

"'He has shown King Nebuchadnezzar what will happen in days to come. . . . As you were lying there, O king, your mind turned to things to come, and the revealer of mysteries showed you what is going to happen.'" Daniel 2:28, 29

This must be the foundation of our interpretation: that the dream concerns the future from the time of Nebuchadnezzar onwards; and that it reveals as much of the future as would be of interest to a heathen king. Persecutions of the saints or blasphemies of the anti-Christ are completely outside the scope of this prophecy.

"'You looked, O king, and there before you stood a large statue - an enormous, dazzling statue, awesome in appearance. The head of the statue was made of pure gold, its chest and arms of silver, its belly and thighs of bronze, its legs of iron, its feet partly of iron and partly of baked clay. While you were watching, a rock was cut out, but not by human hands. It struck the statue on its feet of iron and clay and smashed them. Then the iron, the clay, the bronze, the silver and the gold were broken to pieces at the same time and became like chaff on a threshing-floor in the summer. The wind swept them away without leaving a

trace. But the rock that struck the statue became a huge mountain and filled the whole earth.'" Daniel 2:31-35

As Daniel spoke, the statue in all its vast perfection seemed to rise before the king. Fresh and clear the events of his dream came to his mind and he nodded his head in recognition. Only the feet were imperfect.

Clay was the material used by ancient engineers for casting metals. Huram used clay molds for casting bronze objects for the temple.[3] Without special precautions, however, the higher temperatures required by molten iron could cause the mold to shatter, and this is obviously what had happened. The feet of this splendid image were formed of broken fragments of the mold mingled with misshapen lumps of iron.

As the king watched in his dream, a huge rock appeared. There are no rocks on the flat alluvial plains of Babylonia. Babylon was built of brick, and only its statues were made of expensively imported stone. Here perhaps was a memory of Nebuchadnezzar's recent expeditions to Palestine, where the heights and defiles of the Lebanon and Anti-Lebanon mountains must have made a deep impression on his mind. Perhaps some wild tribe had attempted defence by rolling rocks down upon his troops, or perhaps he had witnessed the fall of some rain-loosened boulder as it thrashed its way through the scrub towards the valley floor.

In his dream the stone rolled towards the statue and struck it upon the already weakened feet. When the stone passed the gold, silver, bronze and iron were reduced to tiny fragments that were whirled away by the wind. As in a nightmare Nebuchadnezzar watched the rock grow and expand till it became a mountain that filled his view.

"'This was the dream,'" Daniel declared, *"'and now we will interpret it to the king. You, O king, are the king of kings. The God of heaven has given you dominion and power and might and glory; in your hands he has placed mankind and the beasts of the field and the birds of the air. Wherever they live, he has made you ruler over them all. You are that head of gold.'"* Daniel 2:36-38

Considerable ingenuity has been expended over the years by expositors attempting to explain in what way the tiny Babylonian empire deserved the appellation of "head of gold". The reason has been sought in its wealth or culture or learning. A more obvious explanation has been entirely overlooked. Nebuchadnezzar was an absolute eastern monarch, surrounded from his childhood by flattery and adulation. An interpretation that depicted him as the feet of clay would have been instantly rejected, and would probably have resulted in the death of the interpreter.[4]

God loved this courageous young king, and desired to make Himself known to him. In mercy, and to ensure its acceptance, God adapted His message to the prejudices of the hearer. With considerable satisfaction Nebuchadnezzar heard himself described as the "head of gold", and settled himself to hear the rest of the message with an open mind.

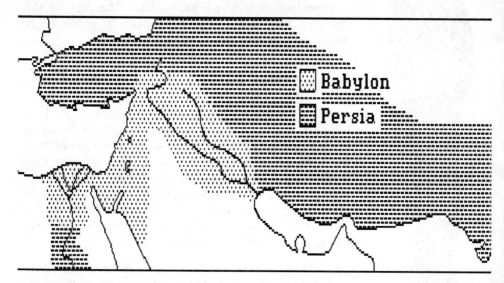

The empires of Babylon and Medo-Persia

"'After you, another kingdom will rise, inferior to yours.'" Daniel 2:39

After Nebuchadnezzar's death the kingdom of Babylon began to decline in strength, but it remained united until it was overthrown by Cyrus of Persia in the year 539 BC. Cyrus defeated the Babylonian army under Nabonidus in a single battle at Opis, near modern Baghdad, and entered Babylon in triumph a few days later.

"'Next, a third kingdom, one of bronze, will rule over the whole earth.'" Daniel 2:39

Under a series of strong rulers, the Persian empire expanded until it stretched from India in the east to Turkey in the west; from the steppes of Russia in the north to Egypt in the south. Despite frequent revolts by ambitious governors, and attacks by savage northern tribesmen, the empire remained a cohesive whole until it was taken over by Alexander the Great.

In revenge for the Persian sack of Athens, Alexander led 35,000 men across the river Granicus in the year 334 BC. A series of victories culminated in the final battle on the plain of Arbela in 331 BC, after which Alexander was undisputed lord of the Persian empire.

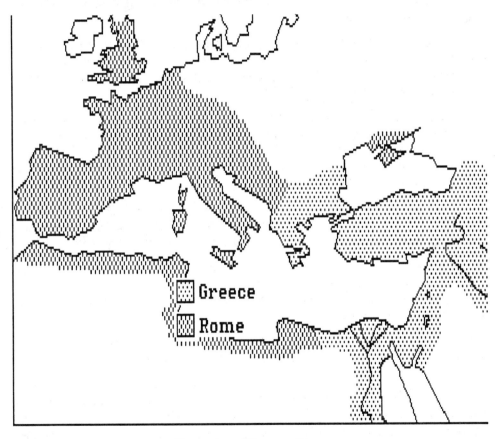

Greece

Rome

The empires of Greece and Rome

" 'Finally there will be a fourth kingdom, strong as iron - for iron breaks and smashes everything - and as iron breaks things to pieces, so it will crush and break all the others.' "
Daniel 2:40

Alexander died after a drunken orgy in Babylon and his kingdom was divided first among his generals and then re-divided among their successors. The highlands of Iran were conquered by the Parthians and India and Afghanistan reverted to their natural chaos, yet despite all this the Greek world retained its distinctive character, a cultural unity that over-rode all other divisions.

This was replaced by the culture of Rome when the legions under Lucius Aemilius Paullus broke the Macedonian phalanx at the Battle of Pydna in 168 BC. Roman roads, Roman law and the Latin tongue ruled the world from the Euphrates to the misty islands of Britain. The ancient tactics of the Carthaginians and the rude fury of the Gauls alike proved ineffective against the ordered discipline of the Romans.

"'Just as you saw that the feet and toes were partly of baked clay and partly of iron, so this will be a divided kingdom; yet it will have some of the strength of iron in it, even as you saw iron mixed with clay. As the toes were partly iron and partly clay, so this kingdom will be partly strong and partly brittle.'" Daniel 2:41, 42

One by one the kingdoms of Babylon, Persia, Greece and Rome succeeded each other. There can be no doubts about the succession. Persia alone conquered Babylon, Greece alone defeated Persia, Rome alone succeeded Greece. When we come to Rome, however, we find a different situation. No one nation or kingdom followed the rule of Rome.

The Roman empire was not conquered by one nation. Over a period of centuries it was broken up and divided between barbarian hordes, swarms of Huns and Herulii, Goths and Vandals, Franks, Alemans and many others.

Yet despite these divisions it could be said that the Roman empire has not come to its end. Our roads still follow the line of the Roman roads, our laws are still based upon the Lex Romana, our languages are a mixture of barbarian speech and the Latin tongue.

"'Just as you saw the iron mixed with baked clay, so the people will be a mixture and will not remain united, any more than iron mixes with clay.'" Daniel 2:43

Although more than one thousand and five hundred years have passed since the barbarians ceased to hammer at the gates of Rome and instead began to hammer at each other in an attempt at unity, all such efforts have failed. Grand political alliances such as the Holy Roman Empire under Charles V of Spain or terrible conquerors such as Charlemagne or Hitler in our own day, have all passed away leaving Europe and the world less united than ever.

Many people look fearfully at the situation of the world today and wonder how it will all end. Will there be some great ideal such as the European

Common Market or some great power such as America, that will bring the world under its sway? God gives us the answer.

"'In the time of these kings, the god of heaven will set up a kingdom that will never be destroyed, nor will it be left to another people. It will crush all these kingdoms and bring them to an end, but it will itself endure for ever. This is the meaning of the vision of the rock cut out of a mountain, but not by human hands - a rock that broke the iron, the bronze, the clay, the silver and the gold to pieces.'" Daniel 2:44, 45

There will never be another universal kingdom until God brings in His kingdom of peace and righteousness. We are living in the time when this kingdom is to come about: Babylon has passed away, Persia is gone, Greece no longer rules the world and Rome's legions have turned to dust. Today is the "time of these kings", and God's kingdom, long delayed though it has been, is soon to be established on earth.

"'The great God has shown the king what will take place in the future. The dream is true and the interpretation is trustworthy.'" Daniel 2:45

Those who love God, and eagerly await the kingdom He has promised, will take hope from these words. Only the wicked, the cruel, the selfish, will reject the promise and look towards its fulfilment with fear. Nebuchadnezzar recognised the dream and accepted the interpretation.

"Then King Nebuchadnezzar fell prostrate before Daniel and paid him honour and ordered that an offering and incense be presented to him. The king said to Daniel, 'Surely your God is the God of gods and the Lord of kings and a revealer of mysteries, for you were able to reveal this mystery.'" Daniel 2:46

Far more than foretelling the future, God wanted to reveal Himself to Nebuchadnezzar. Together with God, this new kingdom and its intelligent young king could become a tremendous power for good in the world. For a while it seemed that God's plan would succeed.

"Then the king placed Daniel in a high position and lavished many gifts on him. He made him ruler over the entire province of Babylon and placed him in charge of all its wise men. Moreover, at Daniel's request the king appointed Shadrach, Meshach and Abed-nego

administrators over the province of Babylon, while Daniel himself remained at the royal court." Daniel 2:48, 49

---

1. In common with most other countries of the Middle East, the Babylonians calculated the years of a king's reign from one New Year's Day to the next. In consequence a king might reign as much as 11 months before the start of the first official year of his reign.

2. Like other books of the Old Testament, the first part of the book of Daniel is written in Hebrew. From the word "Aramaic" onwards it changes to Aramaic, the court and diplomatic language of the Middle East. At the beginning of chapter 8 the author reverts to Hebrew. Only Ezra, another book from the period of the captivity, shares this peculiarity of being written in two languages.

3. 2 Chronicles 4:17

4. Some may object that God does not stoop to such methods to reach men. In fact God is willing to use any method that will allow His messages to break through the barriers of human prejudice. Isaiah walked naked for three years, Hosea was told to marry a prostitute and Ezekiel lived on a starvation diet for over a year, all to dramatise God's call to national repentance.

DANIEL

Chapter 3

For three years Nebuchadnezzar led his armies into Palestine to collect tribute and to impress the might and power of Babylon on the petty states and kinglets. Remaining centres of Egyptian power such as Askelon were subdued without provoking a reaction from Egypt.

In the year 601 BC the Egyptians once more marched through Palestine and north to the vital river crossings. Nebuchadnezzar had grown confident and careless and Pharaoh Necho caught him unprepared. The ensuing battle was a severe defeat for the Babylonians - so severe that the following year Nebuchadnezzar had to stay at home rebuilding his shattered army.

With Pharaoh's forces ranging freely over the land, the small nations of Palestine had perforce to declare for Egypt. The next year's tribute went south instead of north and Jehoiakim, king of Judah, settled down happily to being part of the Egyptian empire.

"During Jehoiakim's reign Nebuchadnezzar king of Babylon invaded the land and Jehoiakim became his vassal for three years. But then he changed his mind and rebelled against Nebuchadnezzar." 2 Kings 24:1

It seemed that the brief period of Babylonian power had come to an end and that the kingdom of silver was about to enter upon the scene. For a short time Daniel must have been an object of superstitious interest to the people of Babylon. Nebuchadnezzar alone determined that his dream of the image should not come true.

While he could not lead his depleted forces to another battle, Nebuchadnezzar could use his wealth to foment unrest in the region. As so often both before and since, the great powers used the Arab tribes as tools in their own political quarrels.

"The Lord sent Chaldean, Aramean, Moabite and Ammonite raiders against him." 2 Kings 24:2

Encouraged by Babylonian gold and Babylonian military advisers, the tribes and nations east of the Jordan engaged in terrorism. Small groups of raiders crept across the Jordan by night, attacked a village or small town at dawn and then disappeared back into the desert before the local defence forces could be organised.

Even as he took these steps to protect his position abroad, Nebuchadnezzar evolved a bold plan to raise morale at home and to put an end to the defeatist whispers that centred on the Jewish captive Daniel.

"King Nebuchadnezzar made an image of gold, ninety feet high and nine feet wide and set it up on the plain of Dura in the province of Babylon." Daniel 3:1 [1]

The statue must have been a most impressive sight, towering over the table-top flat plain of Dura, the sun winking off its golden coating as its very presence proclaimed the might and permanence of Babylon's empire. Deliberately Nebuchadnezzar set out to attack and challenge the God of heaven. He determined to show that the power and might of Babylon would continue and that no-one need fear the kingdoms of silver, bronze and iron.

On the appointed day Nebuchadnezzar summoned all his officials, the provincial governors, army generals and political advisers, dry lawyers from the justice department and even drier auditors from the treasury. All were assembled on the plain of Dura and then a herald stepped forward.

"'This is what you are commanded to do, O peoples, nations and men of every language: As soon as you hear the sound of the horn, flute, zither,[2] lyre, harp, pipes and all kinds of music, you must fall down and worship the image of gold that King Nebuchadnezzar has set up. Whoever does not fall down and worship will immediately be thrown in a blazing furnace.'" Daniel 3:4

Captive Hebrew musician
from an Assyrian relief.

Behind their bronze shields the Greek mercenaries of Nebuchadnezzar's elite body-guard smiled in derision at the barbarian ceremonies. Certainly they were not afraid of the predictions of such outlandish gods. Nor were they the only ones present who did not reverence the gods of Babylon.

Although some of the gods were common to all the people of Mesopotamia, every city had its own pantheon of gods and goddesses. Worship was thus a political as well as a religious act. Public worship of Nebuchadnezzar's image not only recognised the authority of the conqueror and his gods, but bound the worshipper by solemn religious vows to be loyal. Here was a new god that defied the dream and the God of Israel and at the same time bound the notables of the kingdom in personal loyalty to its creator.

Under these circumstances some might feel justified in performing the outward action of bowing down, acknowledging the political loyalty as required without compromising their personal spiritual dedication to the One True God. After all, Nebuchadnezzar was not asking for continued idolatry; just this one demonstration of political opinion.

Against such reasoning stood the uncompromising demand of the Ten commandments.

"You shall not make for yourself an idol in the form of anything in heaven above or on the earth beneath or in the waters below. You shall not bow down to them or worship them." Exodus 20:4, 5

Not only was worship forbidden by the second command but the very act of bowing down or displaying reverence to an image was also prohibited. The royal edict thus presented God's followers with a simple choice - would they obey God exactly or would they obey the king?

At the appointed time the trumpets sounded and the zithers twanged. The whole vast multitude bowed and prostrated themselves except for a lonely group of three young men who stood conspicuously erect - Shadrach, Meshach and Abed-nego.[3]

"At this time some astrologers came forward and denounced the Jews. They said to king Nebuchadnezzar, '. . . There are some Jews whom you have set over the affairs of the province of Babylon - Shadrach, Meshach and Abed-nego - who pay no attention to you, O king. They neither serve your gods nor worship the image of gold you have set up.'" Daniel 3:8, 12

For several years the Chaldeans had smarted over the affair of the king's dream. Far from being grateful for the manner in which their lives were spared, they harboured feelings of bitterness at the admission of impotence that had been forced from them by the king and at the loss of political power that had followed their defeat and the consequent rise of the Hebrew captives.

No doubt they were aware that the Jews were prohibited from idolatry and unfriendly eyes had marked down the spot where the three young men stood, eager to see what they would do. Now they hastened to the king and told him that the three refused to worship his golden image. They represented it as an act of political defiance, saying "They pay no attention to you."

Nebuchadnezzar was furious. It was because of these Jews and their God that he had been obliged to arrange this whole expensive affair. He could not afford to allow them to defy him before the multitude. They, of all people, must bow down - and be seen to bow down - before the image of his state. The three youths were brought before the king.

"Nebuchadnezzar said to them, 'Is it true, Shadrach, Meshach and Abed-nego, that you do not serve my gods or worship the image of gold that I have set up? Now when you hear the sound of the horn, flute, zither, lyre, harp, pipes and all kinds of music, if you are ready to fall down and worship the image I made, very good. But if you do not worship it, you will be thrown immediately into a blazing furnace. Then what god will be able to rescue you from my hand?" Daniel 3:14, 15

The king recognised that their defiance proceeded from religious rather than political motives, but the situation which he himself had created was such that there could be no alternative. He asked for no long-term commitment, they might hold whatever mental reservations they would, but on this occasion they must bend the knee or die.

As an eastern despot, Nebuchadnezzar was accustomed to holding the power of life and death over his subjects. No human power could deliver them if he was determined on their death. No doubt he had often heard the victims of his caprice calling upon their gods for aid. The Babylonians believed that the king was semi-divine; his will was the will of the gods. Practical experience and heathen theology combined to make the king certain that not even a god could deliver the doomed victim from his hands.

Faced with the certainty of death if they refused to obey, many another might have begged for mercy or for time to consider, but the three Hebrews had no need for such deliberation. Long ago, when as helpless hostages they had dared the wrath of the king in the little matter of food and drink, they had made up their minds to obey God. By faithfulness in small, relatively unimportant matters, they had prepared themselves to face the larger test that now confronted them.

"Shadrach, Meshach and Abed-nego replied to the king, 'O Nebuchadnezzar, we do not need to defend ourselves before you in this matter. If we are thrown into the blazing

furnace, the God we serve is able to save us from it, and he will rescue us from your hand, O king. But even if he does not, we want you to know, O king, that we will not serve your gods or worship the image of gold you have set up.'" Daniel 3:16-18

The young men had no assurance that they would be delivered. They knew the power of their God, that He was capable of rescuing them from the furnace, but they were not acquainted with His plans. They did not know if God would deliver them. They recognised that sometimes, for His Own purposes, God allows suffering or death to come to His servants.

Even a human father may have to risk the lives of his children, sometimes for their own good, as when he submits the child to the perils of vaccination or some operation; sometimes for the good of others, as when he sends his sons to battle or on some hazardous voyage. In the same way, God may require His children to risk their lives in His service - and the purposes of this adventure may not be obvious.

Job was called upon to suffer the loss of his possessions and even his children without knowing the reason why his faith was being tested. True children of God, who have learned to trust His love and accept His wisdom, will say like Job:

"Though He slay me, yet will I hope in Him." Job 13:15

Furious at this open defiance, his anger increased by the rejection of his mercy, Nebuchadnezzar passed sentence of death.

"Then Nebuchadnezzar was furious with Shadrach, Meshach and Abed-nego, and his attitude towards them changed. He ordered the furnace to be heated seven times hotter than usual and commanded some of the strongest soldiers in his army to tie up Shadrach, Meshach and Abed-nego and throw them into the blazing furnace. So these men, wearing their robes, trousers, turbans and other clothes, were bound and thrown into the blazing furnace. The king's command was so urgent and the furnace so hot that the flames of the fire killed the soldiers who took up Shadrach, Meshach and Abed-nego, and these three men, firmly tied, fell into the blazing furnace." Daniel 3:19-23

A Mesopotamian furnace or kiln

At this time Nebuchadnezzar was involved in an extensive building programme in Babylon. The alluvial flood-plain of the

Tigris and Euphrates rivers does not have any stone, so all buildings were made of brick, either sun-dried or baked in a kiln. For important buildings such as temples and palaces Nebuchadnezzar used vast quantities of baked bricks, so the furnace on the plain of Dura was probably a brick kiln.

Mesopotamia is rich in oil, which in many places flows freely on the surface and forms pools and rivulets. Even in the time of Nebuchadnezzar the use of oil as a fuel was understood and oil - or oil mixed with chaff - probably provided the fuel for making the furnace seven times hotter.

Although the victims' clothes were usually the perquisite of the executioners, Nebuchadnezzar's fury was so impressive that the soldiers dared not delay, but seized Shadrach, Meshach and Abed-nego, bound them and threw them into the furnace. So intense was the heat coming from the door of the furnace that the soldiers' garments ignited and they died in screaming agony, their armour discoloured by the heat.

The fate of the unfortunate soldiers was quickly forgotten by the onlookers.

"Then King Nebuchadnezzar leaped to his feet in amazement and asked his advisers, 'Weren't there three men that we tied up and threw into the fire?' They replied 'Certainly, O king.' He said, 'Look! I see four men walking around in the fire, unbound and unharmed, and the fourth looks like a son of the gods.'" Daniel 3:24, 25

Through the flames and the shimmering heat the king stared in amazement at the four figures moving about in the cramped interior of the furnace. Three he recognised as the Hebrew youths who had stood so boldly before him but the fourth was so regal in bearing, so majestic in appearance, that he could only liken him to a god-like being.

Heads craned to see what the king saw. The multitude surged as near as they dared, the image forgotten, the band ignored. Trembling and troubled Nebuchadnezzar left his throne and approached the furnace.

"'Shadrach, Meshach and Abed-nego, servants of the Most High God, come out! Come here!' So Shadrach, Meshach and Abed-nego came out of the fire, and the satraps, prefects, governors and royal advisers crowded around them. They saw that the fire had not harmed their bodies, nor was a hair of their head singed; their robes were not scorched, and there was no smell of fire on them." Daniel 3:26, 27

In an attempt to save his pride and dignity Nebuchadnezzar issued a new edict.

"'I decree that the people of any nation or language who say anything against the God of Shadrach, Meshach and Abed-nego be cut into pieces and their houses be turned into piles of rubble, for no other god can save in this way.'" Daniel 3:29

The forgotten image was quietly dismantled, the band and the multitude returned home and the three young men were promoted even higher in the royal service. Once more the city of Babylon rang with praise of the God of Heaven.

When Nebuchadnezzar marched into Palestine and re-captured Jerusalem, his justice was tempered with mercy out of respect for the God of Israel. Although Jehoiakim was killed and his son dethroned, the city was spared and allowed its own king - Zedekiah.

---

1. If this image was in the form of a man then the proportions of 1 across to 10 high are wrong. It is probable therefore that the dimensions given include a base or pedestal.

2. The zither or "kithera" was a Greek instrument. For many years this mention of a Greek instrument was held to prove that a late myth had been incorporated into the book of Daniel. Archaeologists have now discovered that Nebuchadnezzar employed Greek mercenaries in his army and Ionian artisans on his building projects. If he doubted the loyalty of his own people, what more likely than that he appeared on the plain of Dura guarded by his Greek mercenaries and accompanied by their band?

3. Whether Daniel was omitted from the royal command because Nebuchadnezzar's superstitions made him afraid of Daniel's powers or because the king felt certain pangs of conscience at thus boldly defying Daniel's God we cannot say. It may even have been pure chance that caused Daniel to be absent at this time, but we can be sure that he would have acted in the same way as his companions.

DANIEL

Chapter 4

For four years the city states of Palestine survived in precarious independence while Nebuchadnezzar built up his forces, but in the year 597 BC the Babylonians appeared once more in the land of Canaan.

Swiftly Nebuchadnezzar forced the rebellious cities to surrender - even Jerusalem yielded after a three month siege[1] - and King Jehoiachin was taken captive back to Babylon where he was closely confined until his death. In his place Nebuchadnezzar installed a half-brother by the name of Zedekiah.

According to the theology of those days, nations became stronger or weaker according as their patron deities were ranked in the hierarchy of heaven. Defeated kings were forced to swear their oaths of allegiance by the conqueror's gods, for these were obviously the stronger and more potent.

It is all the more significant, therefore, that when Zedekiah took his coronation oath and swore fealty to Nebuchadnezzar, he swore by the God of Heaven.

"Zedekiah was twenty-one years old when he became king, and he reigned in Jerusalem for eleven years. He did evil in the eyes of the Lord his God and did not humble himself before Jeremiah the prophet, who spoke the word of the Lord. He also rebelled against King Nebuchadnezzar, who had made him take an oath in God's name." 2 Chronicles 36:11-13

The unprecedented privilege of swearing by a defeated god is the measure of the impact made on Nebuchadnezzar by the loyalty of the Hebrew youths and by their miraculous deliverance from the blazing furnace. The tragedy was that Zedekiah had no real reverence for the God he worshipped and when it suited him politically he broke his oath and rebelled against Babylon.

Nebuchadnezzar's response was swift and terrible. He besieged Jerusalem and captured it in 586 BC, then gave special orders to his army general:

"On the seventh day of the fifth month in the nineteenth year of Nebuchadnezzar king of Babylon, Nebuzaradan commander of the imperial guard, an official of the king of Babylon, came to Jerusalem. He set fire to the temple of the Lord." 2 Kings 25:8, 9

The temple built by Solomon was completely destroyed and the nation of Israel ceased to exist. This reversal of Nebuchadnezzar's former tolerance was an act of defiance against the God of heaven, a God Who was sufficiently powerful to deliver His servants from the flames of the furnace, but was unable or unwilling to keep His servants faithful to their oaths.

At the same time the influence of the Hebrews vanished. A Babylonian court almanac for the year 570 BC makes no mention of Daniel or his friends, indicating that Zedekiah's treachery had cost them the high posts they held in Babylon.

Nebuchadnezzar turned back to the old gods, and set about building a city and temples to their glory. As far away as Ur, Leonard Woolley found evidence for Nebuchadnezzar's building activities, and the changes he made in the forms of worship.[2]

But although Nebuchadnezzar had turned his back on the God of heaven, God had not forsaken him. Towards the end of his reign God sent him a special message of warning and reproof. The story is told in the king's own words:

"I, Nebuchadnezzar, was at home in my palace, contented and prosperous. I had a dream that made me afraid." Daniel 4:4

In unconscious re-enactment of the events nearly thirty years before, Nebuchadnezzar sent first for the astrologers and priests of Babylon. Once again these wise men had to confess that they could not understand the symbolism of the dream.

"Finally, Daniel came into my presence and I told him the dream." Daniel 4:8

Nebuchadnezzar's dream concerned a tree which gave shelter and food to the whole world. As he gazed upon it a voice rang out from the sky:

" 'Cut down the tree and trim off its branches; strip off its leaves and scatter its fruit. Let the animals flee from under it and the birds from its branches. But let the stump and its roots, bound with iron and bronze, remain in the ground, in the grass of the field. Let him be drenched with the dew of heaven and let him live with the animals among the plants of the

earth. Let his mind be changed from that of a man and let him be given the mind of an animal, till seven times pass by for him. The decision is announced by messengers, the holy ones declare the verdict, so that the living may know that the Most High is sovereign over the kingdoms of men and gives them to anyone he wishes and sets over them the lowliest of men.'" Daniel 4:14-17

As soon as he heard the dream Daniel grasped its significance. For the last decade or more Nebuchadnezzar had been undisputed lord of the Middle East. Tyre had yielded after a thirteen year siege; Egypt had been plundered in a brief raid; even far-away Persia and Lydia had accepted Nebuchadnezzar's arbitration in their dispute through the person of his protege Nabonidus.

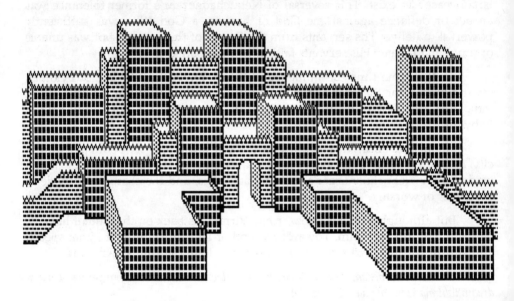

The Ishtar Gateway of Babylon

The wealth of all the world flowed into Babylon and Nebuchadnezzar had spent freely in making Babylon the most beautiful of cities. Temples and palaces adorned its wide streets; the enormous banqueting hall seated a thousand guests and the fabulous hanging gardens had been erected to satisfy the whim of his Median wife. Stout bridges spanned the Euphrates and a broad double wall of burnt brick surrounded the whole to provide impregnable security for both king and capital.

Nebuchadnezzar could look over his city and be justly proud of what he had accomplished. But with pride had come arrogance. The young prince who had worshipped the God of heaven thirty years before had been replaced by a hard, cynical ruler who enforced his will with an iron hand and punished those who displeased him with terrible severity.

For a long while Daniel stood silent, for he knew that what he had to say would not be pleasing to the king. As a human being he may even have quailed at the prospect of upsetting the capricious tyrant before him.

"Then Daniel (also called Belteshazzar) was greatly perplexed for a time, and his thoughts terrified him. . . . Belteshazzar answered, 'My lord, if only the dream applied to your enemies and its meaning to your adversaries! . . . You, O king, are that tree! You have become great and strong; your greatness has grown until it reaches the sky and your dominion extends to distant parts of the earth.'" Daniel 4:19-22

With tactful words Daniel began his interpretation. Once more the king's dream concerned the future but this time his own future. The God of heaven was about to punish the pride of the king and doom swiftly approached.

Daniel knew that God's promises and His threatenings are alike conditional. He knew that this dream was given to the king to warn him so that the punishment might be averted.

"If I tell the righteous man that he will surely live but then he trusts in his righteousness and does evil, none of the righteous things he has done will be remembered; he will die for the evil he has done. And if I say to the wicked man, 'You will surely die' but he then turns away from his sin and does what is just and right . . . he will surely live; he will not die." Ezekiel 33:13-16

"I take no pleasure in the death of the wicked," God declares, *"but rather that they turn from their ways and live. Turn! Turn from your evil ways! Why will you die?" Ezekiel 33:11*

With plain and simple words Daniel warned Nebuchadnezzar of the fate that was in store for him, and then, in one of the most remarkable pleas for repentance ever recorded, Daniel begged the king:

"'Therefore, O king, be pleased to accept my advice: Renounce your sins by doing what is right and your wickedness by being kind to the oppressed. It may be that then your prosperity will continue.'" Daniel 4:27

Nebuchadnezzar listened in astonishment. No one had ever spoken to him like this before. Daniel's words and the earnestness with which they were spoken convinced him of the need for reformation in his life.

For a time there was indeed a change in Nebuchadnezzar. For a whole year, by the exercise of an iron will, he laid aside his arrogance and his cruelty; but he failed to do the most important thing.

"Can the Ethiopian change his skin or the leopard its spots? Neither can you do good who are accustomed to doing evil." Jeremiah 13:23

Nebuchadnezzar failed to worship the God of heaven and seek His help. No one, in their own strength, can overcome man's innate tendency to evil. By the exercise of his will Nebuchadnezzar curbed his arrogance, but the underlying pride and selfishness remained, unrecognised and unchanged.

There is only one solution to the problem of man's weak, human tendencies and that is to allow the God of heaven to change man's basic nature. God promises:

"I will give you a new heart and put a new spirit in you; I will remove from you your heart of stone and give you a heart of flesh. And I will put my spirit in you and move you to follow my decrees and be careful to keep my laws." Ezekiel 36:26, 27

Only by opening himself to the God of heaven could Nebuchadnezzar hope to bring about a real and lasting change in himself, but this was the one thing he failed to do. Time passed and as the threatened punishment failed to materialise Nebuchadnezzar became less guarded in his behaviour, less careful of his words and thoughts.

"All this happened to King Nebuchadnezzar. Twelve months later, as the king was walking on the roof of the royal palace of Babylon, he said, 'Is not this the great Babylon I have built as the royal residence, by my mighty power and for the glory of my majesty?'

"The words were still on his lips when a voice came from heaven, 'This is what is decreed for you, King Nebuchadnezzar: Your royal authority has been taken from you. You will be driven away from people and will live with the wild animals; you will eat grass like cattle. Seven times will pass by for you until you acknowledge that the Most High is sovereign over the kingdoms of men and gives them to anyone he wishes.'" Daniel 4:28-32

A dreadful change came over the king. Suddenly he began to issue garbled commands, ordering wholesale executions of the nobility, the desecration of temples, the destruction of cities. When the appalled courtiers failed to obey instantly, he raved at them, foaming at the mouth, growling and biting, striking wildly at anyone who approached him.

A recently translated cuneiform tablet found in the British Museum describes Nebuchadnezzar's behaviour during his madness. "His life appeared of no value to him . . . then he gives an entirely different order . . . he does not show love to son and daughter . . . family and clan does not exist."[3]

Unfortunately this tablet is very damaged and most lines are broken. It mentions that "bad counsel" is given to Evil-Merodach, Nebuchadnezzar's son but does not tell us the source of this "bad counsel". Perhaps he was urged to take the throne in place of his father. Knowing the cause and the duration of the

A cuneiform tablet

king's malady, Daniel would have opposed this and the feeling of the populace was on his side.

In the east people believed that madness occurred when a god took possession of a person's mind. Although they might take steps to protect themselves and their property against the mania of the lunatic, they dared not attempt to destroy the god within the person, nor would anyone try to take advantage of his position lest they draw the wrath of the gods upon themselves.

It was obvious to the people of Babylon that some god had taken control of Nebuchadnezzar's mind. They dared not imprison or restrain him lest they restrict the god and provoke its anger, so they contented themselves with driving him out into the open fields where his frantic behaviour could harm no one but himself.

"Immediately what had been said about Nebuchadnezzar was fulfilled. He was driven away from people and ate grass like cattle. His body was drenched with the dew of heaven until his hair grew like the feathers of an eagle and his nails like the claws of a bird." Daniel 4:33

For seven years a council of princes and nobles held the kingdom in trust for their king. In all that time Nebuchadnezzar showed no signs of intelligence, but wandered alone and uncared for through the fields and marshes of Babylonia. At the end of that time the tablet records: "He prays to the Lord of lords, he raises his hands in supplication." The Bible records the king's own words.

"At the end of that time, I, Nebuchadnezzar, raised my eyes towards heaven, and my sanity was restored. Then I praised the Most High; I honoured and glorified Him Who lives for ever. His dominion is an eternal dominion; His kingdom endures from generation to generation. All the peoples of the earth are regarded as nothing. He does as He pleases with the powers of heaven and the peoples of the earth." Daniel 4:34, 35

With terrible clarity Nebuchadnezzar saw himself as he really was - a mortal man, no greater, except as God had blessed him, than any other. He saw himself as a creature, owing health, wealth, reason and life itself to his Maker. It is given to few men to thus see their true condition and then to humble themselves before the Almighty.

God our Creator demands our obedience and submission and this it is our duty to give. We have nothing of which to be proud. All our wealth and wisdom and accomplishments have come to us, directly or indirectly, from Him and as Nebuchadnezzar discovered, they can be as easily and as rapidly withdrawn.

Our only worth is the value that our Maker places upon us. Fortunately, that value is infinite.

"For God so loved the world that he gave his one and only Son, that whoever believes in him shall not perish but have eternal life." John 3:16

God does not want to destroy or punish us. He wants to make us fit for immortal life in a perfect universe. Only obedience to His far greater intelligence and wisdom can make us trustworthy citizens of that new world. Deliberate disobedience, even in things which we might consider small and unimportant, shows that we place our own inclinations before God's will; we are only obedient when God's will co-incides with ours.

"At the same time that my sanity was restored, my honour and splendour were returned to me for the glory of my kingdom. My advisers and nobles sought me out, and I was restored to my throne and became even greater than before. Now I, Nebuchadnezzar, praise and exalt and glorify the King of heaven, because everything he does is right and all his ways are just. And those who walk in pride He is able to humble." Daniel 4:36, 37

---

1. Thanks to the Babylonian Chronicle, translated by D. J. Wiseman of the British Museum, this date is securely fixed in history. Indeed, our information is so precise that we are able to say that Jerusalem surrendered on Saturday, March 16, 597 BC.

2. Woolley, Excavations at Ur, 1954. p. 228

3. BM 34113

DANIEL

Chapter 5

Nebuchadnezzar died in 562 after a reign of forty-three years and with him died the Babylonian empire. A series of weak and immoral kings kept it in being for another twenty-three years but they were years of decline and decay. Nebuchadnezzar was succeeded by his son Amel-Marduk, who is called Evil-Merodach in the Bible.

"In the thirty-seventh year of the exile of Jehoiachin king of Judah, in the year Evil-Merodach became king of Babylon, he released Jehoiachin from prison on the twenty-seventh day of the twelfth month. He spoke kindly to him and gave him a seat of honour higher than those of the other kings who were with him in Babylon. So Jehoiachin put aside his prison clothes and for the rest of his life ate regularly at the the king's table. Day by day the king gave Jehoiachin a regular allowance as long as he lived." 2 Kings 25:27-29

Of course Jehoiachin had been in receipt of official rations ever since his capture. Cuneiform tablets from 592 BC list the payment of oil, barley and other provisions to captives and skilled craftsmen. "Yaukin", king of Judah, and five of his sons are among those who received these rations. It seems that for some reason Amel-Marduk showed particular favour to Jehoiachin in the same way as King David showed favour to Mephibosheth.[1]

Because Nebuchadnezzar held the reins of government so tightly in his own hands Amel-Marduk had lived a life of idleness and dissipation at his father's court. These evil habits continued after he ascended the throne and so disgusted the court that a conspiracy was formed against him. After less than two years on the throne he was murdered and Nergal-Shar-Usur became king in 560 BC.

The new king was one of Nebuchadnezzar's most honoured courtiers.[2] As a mark of favour, Nergal-Shar-Usur had been given one of Nebuchadnezzar's daughters as a wife and he was therefore related to the royal line of descent.

Although Nergal-Shar-Usur was an old man, he ruled vigorously, leading campaigns in Cilicia and against rebels - whom he burnt to death. He also undertook an extensive building program. He died after a short reign of four years and was succeeded by his son Labashi-Marduk.

The unfortunate Labashi-Marduk did not find favour with the powerful clique of courtiers who controlled the succession and after a mere two months as king he was seized and tortured to death. The conspirators selected a man called Nabonidus as the next king.

The story of Nabonidus' life is interesting: his mother's name was Shamua-Damqa, a priestess of the moon-goddess Nin in the city of Haran. His father, Nabu-Balatsu-Iqbi, was an Assyrian prince of that city. When Haran was captured by the Medes and Babylonians in 610 BC the prince of the city was killed and Shamua-Damqa and her son were taken to Babylon.

In Babylon the good-looking young captive was taken into Nebuchadnezzar's harem and in due course rose to become one of his favourite wives. Her son shared Nebuchadnezzar's favour and was employed by him in a number of sensitive missions, including an attempt at mediation between the Medes and the Lydians in 585 BC. The attempt was successful, mainly due to a total eclipse of the sun which halted the battle and convinced the antagonists that the gods desired peace.

Historical records indicate that Nabonidus married Nitocris, one of Nebuchadnezzar's daughters by an Egyptian princess. By her he had a son whom he named Bel-Shar-Usur or Belshazzar[3] as he is called in the Bible. Belshazzar was thus the grand-son of Nebuchadnezzar on his mother's side.

Nabonidus became king in 556 BC and immediately offended the priests of Marduk in Babylon by showing a marked preference for Nin, the goddess of Haran. Rather than risk assassination amid the intrigues of the court, Nabonidus spent much of his reign outside Babylon, displaying a particular fondness for Haran.

In the year 553 BC Nabonidus was campaigning in Palestine when he fell seriously ill. He was taken to the cool Lebanon mountains and while there, to prevent any conflict arising over the succession, he made his son Belshazzar king. Contrary to expectations Nabonidus then recovered.

Rather than "dethrone" his son, Nabonidus was content to leave him as king of the city and province of Babylon. He himself led his army south to the oasis of Tema in northern Arabia, conquered it and remained there for eleven years. Possibly this was an attempt to find new resources for the Babylonian economy or to open up new trade routes.

During these upheavals at the top of Babylonian society Daniel, once so prominent in that society, seems to have retired very much into the background. Naturally he would have no part in intrigues and conspiracies and he was therefore out of favour with the factions at court.

His fellow Jewish captives led quiet lives, resigned to their fate. Yet they never lost hope. A profound revolution took place among them as they realised that the captivity had come upon them because of idolatry. Now they turned whole-heartedly to the God of heaven. Idolatry never again troubled Israel.

As part of this reformation people studied the law of God given to Moses and the writings of the prophets who called the nation back to the law. In particular they studied the writings of the most recent prophets who had predicted the captivity in Babylon. Among these were the writings of the prophet Isaiah.

The earlier part of Isaiah's book denounces the sins of Israel and proclaims God's judgements against her.

"Stop bringing meaningless offerings! Your incense is detestable to me. New Moons, Sabbaths and convocations - I cannot bear your evil assemblies." Isaiah 1:13

"Woe to those who make unjust laws, to those who issue oppressive decrees. . . . What will you do on the day of reckoning when disaster comes from afar?' Isaiah 10:1, 3

"Woe to the wreath, the pride of Ephraim's drunkards." Isaiah 28:1

"Woe to you, Ariel, Ariel, the city where David settled!" Isaiah 29:1

In contrast, the second part of the book foretells deliverance for God's people - deliverance from Babylon - and even names the deliverer. In chapter 44 God identifies Himself as the God Who can do all manner of difficult things, among them drying up the sea and rebuilding Jerusalem.

". . . . Who says of Cyrus, 'He is my shepherd and will accomplish all that I please; he will say of Jerusalem, "Let it be rebuilt," and of the temple, "Let its foundations be laid."'" Isaiah 44:25

In the same year that Belshazzar was appointed king of Babylon a Persian prince named Cyrus rose in revolt against Astyges, his Median overlord who was also his grandfather. Twice defeated, he achieved victory when the Median commander Harpagus, who had been maltreated by Astyges, deserted to him.

Since then Cyrus had continued to increase in power, campaigning in both east and west. In 547 BC he attacked Lydia and conquered it, capturing King Croesus and his legendary riches. It was obvious what his next target would be.

To the Jews in Babylon the amazing rise of this Persian king was a source of intense interest and hope. Eagerly they studied the scrolls of Isaiah, seeking to discover whether this Cyrus was the promised deliverer. Inevitably word of their speculations came to the attention of the Babylonians and may even have had a significant effect on their morale.

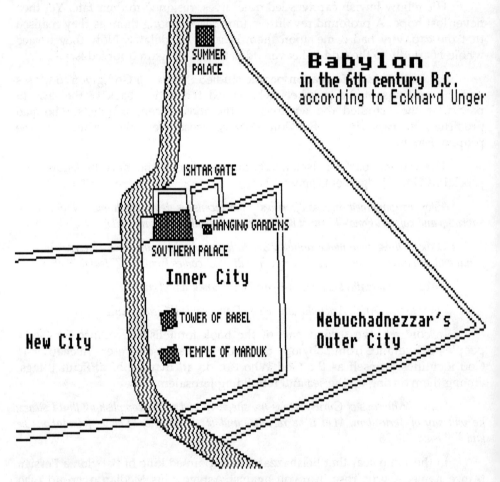

Outline of the city of Babylon

As the crisis deepened Nabonidus returned from Tema and together the two kings, father and son, planned for the defence of their kingdom. Unfortunately, years of absentee government had alienated the powerful nobility and the nation. When Cyrus finally attacked in 539 BC the rich eastern province of Gutium fell with hardly a blow struck.

Nabonidus' immediate reaction was to send and "arrest" all the gods and goddesses of Mesopotamia, bringing them to Babylon and holding them hostage for the continued loyalty of their cities. Then he summoned his armies and marched out to confront Cyrus near the city of Opis.

The battle was a disaster for the Babylonians. Nabonidus was forced to flee to the south, and the Persians were free to settle down and besiege Babylon. Babylon was extremely well defended thanks to Nebuchadnezzar's foresight, and it was well supplied with provisions. Neither Nabonidus nor Belshazzar were unduly concerned by the prospect of a siege.

It so happened that the night of October 11 was one of the great religious festivals of Babylon. To avoid offending the gods, and at the same time to show his confidence in the defences of the city, Belshazzar decided to celebrate the festival with more than usual pomp.

"King Belshazzar gave a great banquet for a thousand of his nobles and drank wine with them." Daniel 5:1

The feast was in itself an act of defiance, mocking Cyrus' futile attempt to besiege a city so well supplied with food. As the banquet progressed the gods of those cities which had surrendered to Cyrus were mocked and insulted and it suddenly occurred to the drunken king to show his contempt for the God of the Jews.

"While Belshazzar was drinking his wine, he gave orders to bring the gold and silver goblets that Nebuchadnezzar his father had taken from the temple in Jerusalem, so that the king and his nobles, his wives and his concubines might drink from them." Daniel 5:2

Although Nebuchadnezzar had burnt the temple of Jerusalem in a deliberate act of defiance against the God of the rebellious Jews, he had retained the sacred vessels in his treasury, guarding them against profane and common use. Thus far he had respected the God of heaven.

Now Belshazzar determined to desecrate these sacred objects by using the goblets for his feast and allowing his concubines to drink from them. Thus he would show his defiance against the God of heaven; thus he would set at nought the rumoured prophecies that pointed to Cyrus and the fall of Babylon.

"So they brought in the gold goblets that had been taken from the temple of God in Jerusalem and the king and his nobles, his wives and his concubines drank from them. As they drank the wine, they praised the gods of gold and silver, of bronze, iron, wood and stone." Daniel 5:3, 4

Many of those attending this feast had also been present on the plain of Dura when three young Hebrews refused to bow to the god of gold that Nebuchadnezzar set up. Many of them had seen Nebuchadnezzar wandering in his madness twenty five years before and had known the reason for it. Yet in their drunken frenzy not one spoke up to protest against the king's sacrilegious folly.

They were unaware that the God Who had so signally worked to glorify His name by delivering the three Hebrew youths and to bring down the pride of a king, was still in control of events. As they raised the golden cups in praise of their idols, the living God moved to uphold His honour.

"Suddenly the fingers of a human hand appeared and wrote on the plaster of the wall, near the lampstand in the royal palace. The king watched the hand as it wrote. His face turned pale and he was so frightened that his knees knocked together and his legs gave way." Daniel 5:5, 6

"Mene, tekel upharsin"

In an instant the revelry and mirth ceased. Belshazzar and his court were so used to their gods of stone and wood, who neither moved nor spoke, that the irruption of the supernatural into their lives left them shocked and trembling. Pale with terror Belshazzar sent for the priests of the state religion, the specialists in the supernatural, and commanded them to read the unknown writing whose fiery glow hung upon the walls.

"The king called out for the enchanters, astrologers and diviners to be brought and said to these wise men of Babylon, 'Whoever reads this writing and tells me what it means will be clothed in purple and have a gold chain placed around his neck, and he will be made the third highest ruler in the kingdom.'" Daniel 5:7

These was no higher position that Belshazzar could offer, for he himself was the second ruler. Anxiously the king and his guests watched as the wise men peered at the wall and consulted with each other. We do not know what the writing looked like. Perhaps the script was strange to the Chaldeans or perhaps God laid His hand over their eyes. At length the men turned away and their spokesman admitted that they were unable to read the writing, nor to guess at its meaning.

"So King Belshazzar became even more terrified and his face grew more pale. His nobles were baffled." Daniel 5:9

As the panic spread it eventually reached even into the harem, and one of the old women who heard the story suddenly remembered another time sixty-four years before when the fathers and grandfathers of these wise men had also been baffled. The Bible identifies this woman as the queen mother, so perhaps she was Shamua-Damqa, the princess of Haran, wife of Nebuchadnezzar and mother of Nabonidus.

Greatly daring she came into the huge hall and approached the drunken youth who now held the throne. Scornfully she reminded him that his father, the great Nebuchadnezzar, had appointed Daniel as chief of the sacred college.

"'Call for Daniel, and he will tell you what the writing means.'" Daniel 5:12

Messengers raced through the night and roused the old man from his sleep. Hastily Daniel dressed and and accompanied them back to the banqueting hall where the king still sat, his bulging eyes riveted by the letters on the wall before him. Belshazzar roused himself and repeated the dazzling offer of riches and honour if Daniel could read the writing.

Daniel looked with distaste on the drunken king and the debauched nobility. With contempt he dismissed the promised rewards.

"Then Daniel answered the king, 'You may keep your gifts for yourself and give your rewards to someone else. Nevertheless, I will read the writing for the king and tell him what it means.'" Daniel 5:17

Solemnly the aged prophet reminded Belshazzar of the greatness and absolute power of his ancestor, Nebuchadnezzar. He repeated the story of Nebuchadnezzar's madness, the punishment which had continued until he acknowledged the greater power of the God of Heaven.

"'But you his son, O Belshazzar, have not humbled yourself, though you knew all this. Instead, you have set yourself up against the Lord of heaven. You had the goblets from His temple brought to you, and you and your nobles, your wives and your concubines drank wine from them. You praised the gods of silver and gold, of bronze, iron, wood and stone,

which cannot see or hear or understand. But you did not honour the God Who holds in His hand your life and all your ways.'" Daniel 5:22, 23

Daniel turned away from the king and in a voice like the voice of doom read out the fatal words.

"'Mene, Tekel, u Pharsin.'" Daniel 5:25

The words were all Aramaic words, and all were in everyday use referring to weights. A mina was about one and a quarter pounds, a tekel or shekel was about four ounces and peres, (the singular of parsin) which means "half" was a half shekel or a half mina.

Each word also had another meaning: "count", "weigh" and "divide". It was on these other meanings that Daniel based his interpretation.

"'This is what these words mean: Mene: God has numbered the days of your reign and brought it to an end. Tekel: You have been weighed on the scales and found wanting. Peres: Your kingdom is divided and given to the Medes and Persians.'" Daniel 5:26-28

As sentence was pronounced the more timorous began to steal away from the fateful hall. To save face before his courtiers, Belshazzar insisted upon presenting the prophet with the royal gifts he had promised, but even as he proclaimed Daniel third ruler in the kingdom, that kingdom was passing away.

Some miles upstream from Babylon a former ruler had undertaken sophisticated flood control works. A sluice gate could be opened, diverting the Euphrates river into an extensive marsh, thus lowering the level of the river.

Cyrus guessed that during this night of feasting the great bronze gates that lined the river would remain open to allow easy passage for the revellers. He ordered the sluice gate opened and as soon as the river had fallen enough his soldiers slipped into the river bed and walked around the mighty defences that should have kept them out.

At the first bridge across the river they swarmed up the abutments and ran silently towards the gates. Before the drunken guards were aware of them the Persians were masters of the gate and were fanning out through the city, seizing the strategic points almost without resistance.

"This is what the Lord says to his anointed, to Cyrus, whose right hand I take hold of, to subdue nations before him and to strip kings of their armour, to open doors before him so that gates will not be shut: 'I will go before you and will level the mountains; I will break down gates of bronze and cut through bars of iron. I will give you the treasures of darkness, riches stored in secret places, so that you may know that I am the Lord, the God of Israel, who summons you by name.'" Isaiah 45:1-3

Beside the hanging gardens in the centre of Babylon, amidst a huge complex of rooms, halls and passageways stood a vast chamber, 173 feet long, 57 feet wide and 66 feet high. It was the throne room of the southern palace, the only room large enough to hold a thousand guests. Here, surrounded by his bodyguard, Belshazzar attempted to rally his forces.

"That very night Belshazzar, king of the Babylonians, was slain, and Darius the Mede took over the kingdom, at the age of sixty-two." Daniel 5:30, 31

The tragedy of Belshazzar was not that he did wrong, but that he knew better. Degenerate heir to a throne founded upon assassination and intrigue, he nevertheless had before him the example of his grandfather who had wandered in madness for seven years before he acknowledged the God of Heaven.

Although outwardly pious towards his own religion, Belshazzar did not really believe that he would be called to account for his actions. He rejected or ignored such evidences of the supernatural as came his way. It would be too inconvenient and troublesome to subject his desires and ambitions to the will of a Higher Power.

When finally the bloodless finger wrote its words of doom upon the wall before his eyes and he was convinced of the reality of God, it was too late. In place of awe, he could only respond with abject fear; instead of repentance, he could only show bravado.

Too late he honoured the prophet with his pitiful gifts and his empty titles. Weighed and found wanting, he perished and his kingdom passed away.

---

1. 2 Samuel 9:7

2. Jeremiah records that Nergal-Shar-Usur was one of the officials who treated him kindly after his imprisonment in besieged Jerusalem: "So Nebuzaradan the commander of the guard, Nergal-Sharezer a high official and all the other officers of the king of Babylon, sent and had Jeremiah taken out of the courtyard of the guard." Jeremiah 39:13

3. The story of Belshazzar as given here is based upon Babylonian cuneiform records. Both the story and the king were unknown to the Babylonian historian Berossus and to the later Greek and Roman historians. This led many scholars last century to reject Daniel chapter 5 as a late myth and indeed to conclude that the book as a whole dates from the time of the Maccabean revolt. Once again the historical accuracy of the Bible has been triumphantly vindicated and the theories of its critics confounded.

DANIEL

Chapter 6

After the capture of Babylon Cyrus returned to Persia. He left Darius, a Median nobleman, in charge of the conquered empire. Doubtless the appointment was an attempt to gain the favour of the Medes who had been displaced by Cyrus and the Persians.

By the conquest of Babylon Cyrus gained more than just Mesopotamia. He added to his kingdom an area that extended northwards into southern Asia Minor, westwards to the Great Sea and southwards to the border of Egypt. Efficient central government over such an area was clearly impossible, so Darius appointed one hundred and twenty local governors or satraps, responsible in the first instance to three administrators. One of these administrators was Daniel.

There were sound reasons for appointing Daniel to this post. He had been out of favour with the previous administration, which in itself was to his credit. He had a reputation for honesty and uprightness, qualities appreciated by the Persians.

In addition, Daniel was thought to be pro-Persian. His interpretation of the writing on the wall was no doubt reported to the conquerors and Daniel himself may well have shown his new overlords the prophecy of Isaiah which named Cyrus as the deliverer of Israel.

There was, however, one very important reason against his appointment: Daniel was not a Babylonian. The men who took office under the Persians, haughty with the touchy pride of the conquered, could not forget that Daniel had once been their captive. The final straw to their dissatisfaction came when it seemed likely that Daniel would succeed the elderly Darius.

"Now Daniel so distinguished himself among the administrators and the satraps by his exceptional qualities that the king planned to set him over the whole kingdom." Daniel 6:3

Maddened by jealousy, the rival administrators and satraps endeavoured to find some cause of complaint against Daniel. Such an exercise would have been only too easy against any of them for they were all guilty of corruption or oppression, negligent injustice and luxurious living. With Daniel the case was different.

"At this the administrators and the satraps tried to find grounds for charges against Daniel in his conduct of government affairs, but they were unable to do so. They could find no corruption in him, because he was trustworthy and neither corrupt nor negligent." Daniel 6:4

Eventually someone remembered Daniel's strictness over his religion. In the time of Belshazzar and his predecessors it had resulted in Daniel being dismissed from his posts. Now, while it might serve the same purpose, a different approach was necessary.

The Persians were dualists; they believed in Ahura-mazda, the good god of light, and in another evil deity called Ahriman, the god of darkness. This is why, when foretelling the birth and career of Cyrus, God revealed himself as the God of both light and darkness, of good and evil.

"I am Yahweh and there is no other; apart from Me there is no God. . . . I form the light and create darkness, I bring prosperity and create disaster; I, Yahweh, do all these things." Isaiah 45:5, 7

Contrasted with the polytheism of the Babylonians Daniel's strict monotheism commended him to the Persians. The complaint about Daniel's religion needed to be more subtle than a frontal attack.

The conspirators went to Darius and told him that all the governors and administrators, as a mark of their confidence in him, wanted to dedicate the next month to him. For thirty days no other god was to be worshipped, no other man petitioned, apart from Darius himself.

Darius was aware that in the countries over which he ruled the ruler was commonly regarded as divine. Although Darius himself would not have accepted such a superstition he doubtless appreciated the compliment being paid to him and his rule.

He may even have been under orders to give no offence to the gods and religion of his subjects. Cyrus himself had submitted to the age-old ritual of "taking Marduk's hand" when he conquered Babylon, thus making his rule legitimate and his conquest secure.

Perhaps Darius felt pleased, as he pressed his signet to the document, at the thought that at last he had won over the proud Babylonians to accept his rule. It was the last happy moment he was to know for some time.

In an attempt to curb the wilder fancies of despotism, the Medes and Persians had established the custom that edicts issued by the king could not, under any circumstances, be altered or repealed. Aware of this, the crafty Babylonians had stressed the point to Darius, knowing that he would be reluctant to break the rule lest word of his frivolous conduct reach Cyrus' ears.

Whether Daniel was present while this charade was being carried out we do not know. Certainly he knew of the decree very soon after it was made official and quickly realised its implications.

It was Daniel's custom to pray three times a day, kneeling down before an open window facing towards Jerusalem.[1] Although he could not be physically present in the temple, which in any case was now in ruins, Daniel could at least show his faith in the God of Israel by facing towards Jerusalem and the temple when he prayed. In doing this he found peace and hope, guidance for the problems confronting him and strength for the daily task.

Daniel had no intention of suspending his personal devotions because of a royal decree. Neither did he wish it to be thought that he had yielded his conscience to the edict. It would have been easy for him to keep his windows shut or pray from another part of the house, but Daniel scorned to do this. He had served the God of heaven when it was easy and popular to do so and he would continue to serve his God even when it was dangerous and unpopular.

Within minutes the conspirators were gathered outside Daniel's window.

"Then these men went as a group and found Daniel praying and asking God for help. So they went to the king and spoke to him about his royal decree." Daniel 6:11, 12

For a whole day they or their spies watched Daniel to be sure that it was a deliberate act of disobedience, not an excusable lapse of memory, that prompted his actions. Once this was established the conspirators went as a body to the king. Their serious and concerned faces masked inward delight as they reminded Darius of his edict and the penalties that had been laid down. Then in eager voices they made their accusation, using the very same charge their ancestors had made at the time of the fiery furnace.

"Then they said to the king, 'Daniel, who is one of the exiles from Judah, pays no attention to you, O king, or to the decree you put in writing. He still prays three times a day.'" Daniel 6:13

Too late Darius realised that these men had not wanted to honour him but to trap Daniel. In his pride and haste he had become the unwitting instrument for the death of the one man he could trust.

"When the king heard this he was greatly distressed; he was determined to rescue Daniel and made every effort until sundown to save him." Daniel 6:14

The best lawyers in the land were summoned to search for a loophole in the decree, an ambiguity in its terms or an exception to its clauses, but in vain. It had been too carefully drawn up. Its wording was impeccable, its drafting flawless.

As evening fell, under the relentless pressure of hate-driven men, Darius bowed to the inevitable.

"So the king gave the order and they brought Daniel and threw him into the lions' den." Daniel 6:16

From earliest times the rulers of the Mesopotamian countries had enjoyed the pleasures of the chase. Although all wild animals were legitimate prey the greatest thrill and most valued achievement came from killing lions. These were a smaller variety than the huge cats of Africa. Archaeological evidence seems to indicate that they were about the same size as an American puma. Lithe and swift of movement, they were dangerous prey to hunt with primitive weapons such as spears or bow and arrow.

The wholesale depredations of such rapacious hunters as the Assyrian kings had resulted in near extermination of the lions, particularly in the settled environs of great cities like Babylon. The solution was to hold the animals in cages or dens where they could be kept until required for a hunt. Assyrian reliefs depict beasts being transported in cages on sleds and then released at the site chosen for the royal recreation.

Obviously these animals had to be fed, and no doubt the occasional condemned criminal was a welcome change to the standard diet of unwanted offal and unwary pi-dogs, as well as relieving the expenses of the royal exchequer. This was the fate laid down for Daniel.

Guards led the old man from the court towards the royal menagerie and a tearful Darius followed close behind. As the den was uncovered and the feral stench of the wild beasts filled the air Darius forced himself to look at his friend and utter the only words of comfort he could find.

"The king said to Daniel, 'May your God, Whom you serve continually, rescue you!'" Daniel 6:16

They were hollow words and Darius realised their fatuity as soon as he uttered them. Daniel had often spoken to him of the power and might of Yahweh but Darius was a realist. He knew that despite legends and myths the god in whom the Persians believed had never rescued anyone.

The roar of the hungry animals echoed from the underground chamber, mixed with the soft foot-falls of their restless pacing. No power on earth could deliver from their elemental drive for food. With a sinking heart Darius marvelled at his friend's composure.

Gently, because the king was watching, the guards lowered Daniel into the den and dragged the capstone across the opening. Darius and the conspirators sealed the stone in place; an action that for the conspirators ensured that no rescue could reach the doomed man and for Darius meant that no malice could gloat over his death agony.

"Then the king returned to his palace and spent the night without eating and without any entertainment being brought to him. And he could not sleep." Daniel 6:18

Weary and depressed, Darius sat alone in his regal splendour. Food was waved away, musicians and jesters impatiently rejected, the most attractive members of his harem ignored.[2] Through the long hot night Darius mourned for Daniel and as darkness gave way to dawn he could wait no longer.

"At the first light of dawn the king got up and hurried to the lion's den. When he came near the den, he called to Daniel in an anguished voice, 'Daniel, servant of the living God, has your God, whom you serve continually, been able to rescue you from the lions?' Daniel 6:19,20

He didn't really expect an answer to his shouted question. Many another prisoner had been condemned to the same fate and not one had survived the night. Yet, to his amazement, a voice came from beneath the stone.

"Daniel answered, 'O king, live for ever. My God sent His angel and he shut the mouths of the lions. They have not hurt me, because I was found innocent in his sight. Nor have I ever done any wrong before you, O king.'" Daniel 6:21, 22

In incredulous amazement Darius called to the keepers, urging them to haste as they opened the den. Ropes were lowered and Daniel was gently pulled up into the fresh air. King and keepers gazed at him in awe.

"When Daniel was lifted from the den, no wound was found on him, because he had trusted in his God." Daniel 6:23

Although Daniel was convinced that his deliverance was due to the intervention of God's angel, Darius found that explanation too hard to swallow. Gods demanded worship and could be placated with offerings but never in his experience had a god ever concerned itself with the fate of its devotees.

Darius cast about in his mind for an alternative explanation. Remembering that corruption was rife among the effete Babylonians Darius began to wonder if Daniel or his friends had bribed the keepers to feed the lions to repletion before Daniel was placed in the den. He determined to put the matter to the test and gain revenge at the same time.

"At the king's command, the men who had falsely accused Daniel were brought in and thrown into the lions' den, along with their wives and children." Daniel 6:24

With oriental thoroughness Darius included the families of those who had offended him lest a relative be left to take up blood feud against him. Shocked and amazed the conspirators saw Daniel standing unharmed beside the king, then, one by one, they were dragged forward and pushed down into the pit.

"Before they reached the floor of the den, the lions overpowered them and crushed all their bones." Daniel 6:24

Darius watched implacably as shrieking women and pleading men were thrown into the den. Freed of the divine restraint, the hungry beasts leaped and snatched at the bodies that rained down among them. Not one survived, forever dispelling the idea that the lions had not been hungry.

Darius returned to the palace and issued another royal edict, this time directing his kingdom's attention to the God of heaven.

"'I issue a decree that in every part of my kingdom people must fear and reverence the God of Daniel. He is the living God and He endures for ever; He rescues and He saves; He performs signs and wonders in the heavens and on the earth. He has rescued Daniel from the power of the lions.'" Daniel 6:26, 27

It was only a little matter - to pray in public or in private. The edict did not compel Daniel to pray to Darius. He could simply have refrained from prayer for thirty days.

No great question of morality hinged upon Daniel's decision to pray with his windows open. The uncaring multitude in the street below, if they noticed anything, would merely think that for thirty days Daniel had not prayed to his God.

But greater issues were at stake. Had Daniel altered his behaviour to fit the convenience of the day, he would have shown that he served and feared Darius more than he served and loved the God of heaven.

Often today Christians are faced with similar dilemmas - some minor point, some unimportant detail. The world will never notice if they choose the easy path, yet if they stand for right they may suffer loss or hardship, they may face the mockery of friends and relatives.

As Christians we affirm that "Jesus is Lord!" If this is so, how can we place our own convenience or even safety before our duty of obedience to our Lord? When we submit to worldly customs or human traditions we demonstrate that Jesus is not really our Lord.

Daniel honoured his God before the world and in so doing gave God the opportunity to glorify His name. From end to end of the Persian empire men spoke of Daniel's God, Who "rescued Daniel from the power of the lions."

---

1. When Solomon dedicated the newly built temple he had foreseen the possibility of iniquity and exile and besought God "if they turn back to you with all their heart and soul in the land of their enemies who took them captive, and pray to you towards the land you gave their fathers, towards the city you have chosen and the temple I have built for your Name; then from heaven, your dwelling-place, hear their prayer and their plea, and uphold their cause." 1 Kings 8:48, 49

2. The New English Bible renders the phrase "No entertainments" as "No woman was brought to him."

DANIEL

Introduction to Part 2

The first six chapters of Daniel are concerned with the major events of Daniel's life. The remaining six chapters record the visions which Daniel himself received. In order to understand these visions we need to consider two questions: For whom were the messages intended? and How should we interpret the strange symbols of these visions?

The first question is more difficult to answer than we might at first think. Unlike Ezekiel, Daniel's fellow captive, who was given messages to be relayed directly to the Jewish people, there is no indication in the book of Daniel that his visions were to be proclaimed publicly. In fact, the very opposite seems to have been the case.

"'I, Daniel, was deeply troubled by my thoughts, and my face turned pale, but I kept the matter to myself.'" Daniel 7:28

When Ezekiel kept silent after his initial vision he was rebuked by God.

"'Son of man, I have made you a watchman for the house of Israel; so hear the word I speak and give them warning from me.'" Ezekiel 3:17

But not only does Daniel escape reproof for failing to deliver the message; at the end of the book he is told that the words given to him are to be sealed.

"'"But you, Daniel, close up and seal the words of the scroll until the time of the end." . . . *He replied, "Go your way, Daniel, because the words are closed up and sealed until the time of the end."'" Daniel 12:4, 9*

In any case, if God did want to communicate with His people, He could hardly have chosen a less suitable vehicle for His messages. Daniel was already old at the time of his first vision and for most of his life he had lived apart from the bulk of the Jewish nation in exile. As an official at the court of the heathen king he would have been regarded with suspicion and hostility by his fellow captives as a probable collaborator with the enemy.

These considerations lead us to conclude that the visions given to Daniel were not intended for his contemporaries, either Jewish or Babylonian. In fact, we are justified in stating that the visions of Daniel were intended primarily for God's people in the "time of the end", for until that time the words were to be "sealed" and "closed".

Generally, the prophecies of the Bible are "conditional". That is, their fulfilment is dependant upon the behaviour of the people to whom the prophetic word is addressed. Jeremiah stated this principle explicitly:

"If at any time I announce that a nation or kingdom is to be uprooted, torn down and destroyed, and if that nation I warned repents of its evil, then I will relent and not inflict on it the disaster I had planned. And if at another time I announce that a nation or kingdom is to be built up and planted and if it does evil in my sight and does not obey me, than I will reconsider the good I had intended to do for it." Jeremiah 18:7-10

The most obvious case of this principle in practice is that of Jonah, who was sent to Nineveh with the awful message - "Forty more days and Nineveh will be overturned." Yet Nineveh repented and God spared the city - much to Jonah's disgust.

In the same way, Ezekiel predicted the rise of a splendid temple and an ideal city, neither of which ever came true, because the nation failed to serve God and eventually rejected and crucified their Messiah. One of history's greatest questions must be: What if the Jews had accepted Christ?

Daniel, on the other hand, was given visions which he recorded but which were not understood, either by himself or by others, because of the symbols and the convoluted way in which the predictions were made. The visions were intended to benefit people living at the "time of the end".

It follows, therefore, that the visions of the book of Daniel were not conditional visions. While other prophets held out promises of a glorious future - provided the people turned to to God - Daniel spoke of national disaster and the death of the Anointed One. Through Daniel God foretold what would be, while through other prophets He foretold what could be.

It is in this context that we should see God's use of symbols. Many other prophets were directed to use symbols as illustrations of their messages. Ezekiel used the graphic picture of the abandoned baby who proved unfaithful to her benefactor to portray Israel's unfaithfulness to God. Jeremiah smashed a pot in front of the assembled leaders of Jerusalem to depict the completeness of the coming destruction.

In all these cases, however, the symbol was an illustration that heightened the impact of God's message. To fulfil this purpose each symbol was explained in clear and precise terms. This is not the case with the symbols found in Daniel's prophecies.

Although the symbols are explained, the explanation is ambiguous. For example, we are told that the four beasts of chapter seven represent kingdoms, but we are not told which kingdoms. Although both Persia and Greece are named in chapter eight, the horn that followed the four is not identified.

I believe that there were two reasons why God used symbols instead of predicting the future in plain language. The first reason has to do with the manner in which God communicated with Daniel.

A vision is very much akin to a dream: the person experiencing the vision seems to be seeing and hearing events as if they were actually happening around him. It is as if a circuit was established directly into the optic and auditory nerves, by-passing the eyes and ears.

At the conclusion of the vision the prophet "awakens" to the real world about him and then seeks to recall the events he witnessed and the words he heard during his vision. Although the Spirit of God operates to assist the process of recall it is, in fact, a natural process and the prophet describes the vision in his own language.

This is the reason why the first chapter of Ezekiel makes such confusing reading. Ezekiel saw things completely outside his previous experience yet had to describe them in terms of that previous experience.

We are reminded of the often amusing attempts of primitive natives to describe the wonders of 20th century technology. One such described the missionary's organ: "first you walkem feet bilong him, then you punchem teeth bilong him, then he sing out alla same bull moo-cow."

John, in Revelation chapter one, describes Jesus in these words: "His eyes were like blazing fire, His feet were like bronze glowing in a furnace."[1] A modern writer would perhaps use the simile of a searchlight or an arc-lamp. Both would, no doubt, fall short of the glory of the resurrected Lord.

In vision Daniel saw winged lions and four-headed leopards which impressed themselves far more vividly on his mind than a recital of unheard-of names, dates and places would have done. The few words which were spoken he was able to remember, simply because they were so few.

A picture is worth a thousand words and even a word picture can replace a much longer commentary. Daniel saw a winged lion, swift and far-ranging, lose its wings and walk upright in imitation of a man and in that brief vignette graphically and exactly summarised the history of the Babylonian empire.

The second reason is that God wished to make genuine predictions. Imagine a sea-side fortune teller who tells a young girl that she will marry a tall, dark, handsome stranger. A little while later the girl meets a most eligible rich young man but she does not even look at him because he is short and fair and the fortune teller had foretold a tall, dark stranger.

In due course she meets a sunburnt young man of slightly above average height, with modest means and mediocre beauty, yet she marries him. For the rest of her life she sings the praises of the particular clairvoyant: did he not foretell that she would marry a tall, dark, handsome stranger?

You can see that in this case the prediction brought about its own fulfilment. Had God declared in plain language that Babylon would be succeeded by Persia we might suppose that Jews and possibly Babylonians as well would be influenced in one way or another to bring the event about. The Babylonian armies would fight with lesser vigour or the gatekeepers succumb more easily to bribery or intimidation if they thought that Persian victory was inevitable.

On the other hand, it would be possible for someone to read the book of Daniel and then set out to frustrate its predictions. Let us suppose that God had plainly told Daniel that the Messiah would be born on a certain day in a certain town to a certain woman. Herod's minions would have been waiting outside the chamber on the day in question, thankful to have been spared the task of slaughtering a town-full of infants.

For these reasons God chose to cloak his revelations in symbols which would hide their meaning in advance, but which could be clearly recognised after the events had happened. So well did God choose his symbols that commentators agree that the most difficult chapter in the whole book is the one chapter that does not employ symbols - chapter eleven!

With these thoughts in mind, then, let us begin our study of chapter seven.

---

1. Revelation 1:14, 15

DANIEL

Chapter 7

The year 553/2 BC was a portentous one for Mesopotamia. In this year a little known half-Persian called Cyrus rebelled against his grandfather and overlord Astyges. The Medians, who had long ruled the Persians by a mixture of superstition and force, easily shrugged off the threat. What no one could foresee was that within two years a discontented general would go over to Cyrus and the Persians would become the dominant partners in empire.

In Babylon no one was interested in the problems of their erst-while allies. The big talking point was the appointment of Belshazzar as co-regent by his ailing father Nabonidus. For the next eleven years Nabonidus would stay away, governing the empire from the oasis of Tema in northern Arabia while Belshazzar ruled in Babylon and the home provinces.

Yet while the Babylonians ignored the events in the far-away hills of Persia, the warning bell of prophecy rang in Daniel's mind.

"In the first year of Belshazzar king of Babylon, Daniel had a dream and visions passed through his mind as he was lying on his bed. He wrote down the substance of his dream. Daniel said, 'In my vision at night I looked and there before me were the four winds of heaven churning up the great sea.'" Daniel 7:1, 2

Unless Daniel made an unrecorded journey to the Persian Gulf, this vision must have recalled some childhood experience of the Mediterranean, an impression of great wind-driven waves crashing on the sand. As he watched the ceaseless play of wind and water something showed in the foaming surf - a huge animal pulling itself ashore.

" 'The first was like a lion and it had the wings of an eagle. I watched until its wings were torn off and it was lifted from the ground so that it stood on two feet like a man and the heart of a man was given to it.' " Daniel 7:4

At the end of the vision Daniel became aware of others standing on the beach watching the strange procession. Daniel approached one of these and questioned him about the meaning of what he had just seen.

" 'So he told me and gave me the interpretation of these things: "The four great beasts are four kingdoms that will rise from the earth." ' " Daniel 7:15

Amid the storms of human strife, four major powers would dominate the history of God's people. Daniel's thoughts may have gone back through the years to the occasion when, as a young man, he stood before Nebuchadnezzar and told the astonished king of the four kingdoms - gold, silver, brass and iron - that would follow one another before the God of heaven set up His kingdom.

He may even have recognised the identity of the head of gold and the regal lion. Familiar as he was with the winged bulls of Assyria and the composite "sirrush" that adorned the Ishtar gateway, Daniel would not have been at all surprised at the lion's wings or the strange appearance of the other beasts. With grim certainty he would have acknowledged the aptness of the picture as the proud beast's wings were plucked and it was made to walk as a caricature of a man. The sickening intrigues and treachery of the Babylonian court during the last few years were worthy of a harsher judgement.

The next creature was a bear, gory with the remains of its latest kill. Bears are creatures of the hills, not the plains, and were therefore virtually unknown in Mesopotamia. Daniel may have seen bears in the hills of Judea, but no great empire was likely to arise in that direction so his attention may have been drawn to the east, the wild hills of Media and the rising power of Cyrus the Persian.

"'After that I looked and there before me was another beast, one that looked like a leopard. On its back it had four wings like those of a bird. This beast had four heads and it was given authority to rule.'" Daniel 7:6

At this point the meaning of the vision passed beyond the prophet's ken. Even if his thoughts strayed to the bronze clad Greek mercenaries in Nebuchadnezzar's army it is unlikely that he would have linked them with the four-headed leopard. Yet with hindsight we can identify the sure strokes of the political cartoonist - the meteoric rise of Alexander the Great, swift as a leopard, and the equally rapid breakup of his empire (leopards and fowls are swift but without staying power) into the four separate kingdoms of Seleucus, Ptolemy, the Antigonids in Greece itself and the city state of Pergamum in Asia Minor.[1]

"'After that, in my vision at night I looked and there before me was a fourth beast - terrifying and frightening and very powerful. It had large iron teeth; it crushed and devoured its victims and trampled underfoot whatever was left. It was different from all the former beasts and it had ten horns.'" Daniel 7:7

In fascinated horror Daniel watched as the fourth beast rampaged its way across the beach. Then to his amazement, something happened among the ten horns.

"'While I was thinking about the horns, there before me was another horn, a little one, which came up among them; and three of the first horns were uprooted before it. This horn had eyes like the eyes of a man and a mouth that spoke boastfully.'" Daniel 7:8

The shadowy person who interpreted the vision to Daniel commented on the fourth beast.

"'He gave me this explanation: "The fourth beast is a fourth kingdom that will appear on earth. It will be different from all the other kingdoms and will devour the whole earth, trampling it down and crushing it. The ten horns are ten kings who will come from this kingdom. After them another king will arise, different from the earlier ones; he will subdue three kings. He will speak against the Most High and oppress his saints and try to change the set times and the laws. The saints will be handed over to him for a time, times and half a time."'" Daniel 7:23-25

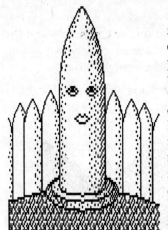

With backward perspective it is not difficult for us to identify the fourth beast as the Roman empire. It was the only unified power to take the place of the Greek empire of Alexander, and though the Parthians ruled the area east of the Euphrates they did not to any significant extent control the destiny of God's people, both Jew and Christian. Furthermore, the fact that the Roman state was ruled by an elected emperor who (in theory at any rate) was the servant of the Senate, marked it out as fundamentally different from the hereditary autocracies that surrounded it.

As in Nebuchadnezzar's dream, the fourth kingdom was not followed by a fifth, but instead of the divided iron and clay Daniel's attention was drawn to the ten horns and especially to the "little horn" which rose among them. "Ten" may be taken as a literal number or more probably in this context as a round number, much as we might use the term "dozen" without meaning an exact twelve. The ten horns which "come from" the fourth empire may therefore be interpreted as the barbarian kingdoms that followed the Roman empire.

What then of the "little horn"? Daniel's description and the explanation of the interpreter give us certain clues to the horn's identity. It came up among the ten, uprooting three of the ten, yet it was different from the ten.[2] It opposed and blasphemed against God, oppressed God's saints, and sought to change God's times and laws. It would be allowed to do all this for a period of three and a half years.[3]

Protestant commentators have uniformly identified this "little horn" as the Roman Catholic church[4], but before adopting this interpretation it is only fair that we consider other possibilities. For example: may we not interpret the "little horn" as the power of Islam?

Although the Arabs came to power after the ten horns were established it could hardly be said that they came up among the ten horns or out of the fourth beast, for the Romans never incorporated Arabia in their empire. An attempt by Aelius Gallus, prefect of Egypt, to conquer Arabia in 24 BC ended in disastrous failure. Further, among all the Muslim conquests, it would be difficult to assign just three kingdoms whose fall was necessary before the Arab Empire could exist.

Turning to the spiritual dimension, it is hard to see how Islam could fit the description of a blasphemous and persecuting power that sought to change God's laws. Muslims honour Jesus (though they do not accept that He was divine) and respect the Bible. Although there have been many pogroms against Christians, the official Muslim stance is one of toleration for Christians and the Christian religion, so much so that in Reformation times members of nonconforming sects fled to the Turks for refuge from Catholic persecution.[5]

Finally, there is no period of three and a half years that is significant in Muslim history. In particular it would be difficult to find such a period when Islam had power over God's laws and saints.

In short, it does not seem possible that Islam can be identified as the "little horn". Other suggestions, such as communism or fascism can be easily rejected in view of their recent origin.

Let us therefore consider the merits of the Protestant position - that the "little horn" is the Roman Catholic church. First we should be clear about one thing: the other horns were kingdoms or political powers. The "little horn" also is identified as a "king" (v. 24) or as a political power. When therefore we speak in this context of the Roman Catholic church we are not referring to the religion as such, nor are we seeking to embarrass the many sincere Christians of the Roman faith.

What we are speaking of is a political power, a combination of religion and politics. This was most characteristic of the medieval papacy, but it was a situation that developed long before the middle ages and continued well after them. We shall use the term "papacy" to denote the religio-political power that is the "little horn".

The papacy certainly grew out of the Roman empire and it attained its political power after the barbarian conquests and while under barbarian rule. Three Arian kingdoms - the Vandals, the Ostrogoths and the Heruli - had to be destroyed before the papacy could achieve full political power because the Arian barbarians persecuted the orthodox Catholics. The first offer of political power to the papacy came from Justinian, the Byzantine emperor, who sought Catholic help in his struggle against the Vandals and the Ostrogoths.

The papacy thus clearly meets the stipulations of the prophecy as far as the circumstances surrounding its rise to power are concerned. What about the manner of its rule?

No one can deny that the papacy was a persecuting power, for the history of the Inquisition, an official instrument of the Church, testifies clearly enough to this fact. Some of its victims were indeed heretics - such as the Albigenses, some were non-Christians - such as the Jews and Moors, and others were fanatics whom any decent person would repudiate - such as the Munster Anabaptists. Yet many were godly folk, sincere Christians, humble followers of Christ, the "saints" of the prophecy.[6]

Many of the popes have been godly men (though misguided, from the Protestant point of view) but there were others who ruled in the Church simply in order to enjoy political power. Such, for example, was the Borgia family whose name has become a synonym for poison and treachery. Along with increasing wealth and temporal power the papacy grasped after spiritual power, accepting titles and attributes that belong to God alone, claiming to be not only the Vicar of Christ but even "another god on earth".[7]

Such exaggerated claims echo Paul's description of the Anti-Christ:

"He will oppose and will exalt himself over everything that is called God or is worshipped, so that he sets himself up in God's temple, proclaiming himself to be God." 2 Thessalonians 2:4

Even if we reject the idea that the papacy is Anti-Christ, we must admit that such claims partake of the spirit of anti-Christ.

In order to bolster its power the papacy claimed the right to alter even the laws of God, appointing or dispensing with feasts, fasts and holy days.

For long the mark of submission to Rome was the acceptance of the Roman Easter. The Roman method of calculating the date of Easter was probably more scientific and accurate than the Jewish ritual that depended upon moonrise over the Mount of Olives, but the difference was not worthy of the significance attached to it by the Roman church. Yet when the churches of Asia Minor clung to the traditional method and refused to adopt the new method Pope Victor (189-198 AD) excommunicated them all as a means of asserting Rome's authority.

The Venerable Bede tells the story of the meeting between Augustine, the Roman missionary to England, and the British bishops, the representatives of the Celtic church.

"Now the Britons did not keep Easter at the correct time, but between the fourteenth and twentieth days of the moon - a calculation depending on a cycle of eighty-four years. Furthermore, certain other of their customs were at variance with the universal practice of the Church. But despite protracted discussions, neither the prayers nor the advice nor the censures of Augustine and his companions could obtain the compliance of the Britons, who stubbornly preferred their own customs. . . . Augustine then declared: 'There are many points on which your customs conflict with ours or rather with those of the universal Church. Nevertheless, if you will agree with me on three points, I am ready to countenance all your other customs although they are contrary to our own. These points are: to keep Easter at the correct time; to complete the Sacrament of Baptism according to the rites of the holy, Roman and apostolic Church; and to join with us in preaching the word of God to the English.'"[8]

Recognising that Easter is a festival established by human custom and tradition, we may view the eventual adoption of the Roman calculation with equanimity. Rome is responsible, however, for a more significant change that has been adopted by Christians at large and which also marks its authority. This change is to the law of God - the Ten Commandments.

The Sabbath day ordained and blessed by God, observed by Jesus and celebrated by the apostolic church was Saturday. As the Hebrew word "shabath" implies, the Sabbath is a day for rest from work, a day on which master and servant, man and wife, parents and children can step aside from the burdens of the week and rejoice with one another and with God. Both Jews and Christians have always been free to worship on any day of the week.

The Sabbath is a memorial to God as the Creator and as such no other day of the week will do. We would think it strange if someone celebrated Good Friday on Wednesday, or New Year's Day on January 2. Bastille Day on July 5 would be a mockery and Christmas Day on December 26, merely for the convenience of shoppers or shopkeepers would deservedly raise an outcry. How then can the anniversary of creation be celebrated on any other day?

Finally, the Sabbath is a continuing testimony to God's Sovereignty. God chose this particular day and no other. No human dispensation or preference can alter God's choice and any attempt to do so is to boldly defy God's holy authority.

Yet, acting as a god on earth, the papacy claims to have changed the Sabbath day from Saturday to Sunday. An official action of the Council of Laodicea in 336 AD recognised a change that had taken place gradually over many years, but which was centred in Rome.

The church historian Socrates (439 AD) tells us:

"Although almost all churches throughout the world celebrate the sacred mysteries on the Sabbath of every week, yet the Christians of Alexandria and at Rome, on account of some ancient tradition, have ceased to do this."[9]

Sozomen, another historian of the same time (440 AD) confirms this.

"The people of Constantinople and almost everywhere, assemble together on the Sabbath, as well as on the first day of the week." He then adds: "This custom is never observed at Rome or at Alexandria."[10]

A modern Roman Catholic apologist has noted this point.

"God said, 'Remember that thou keep holy the Sabbath Day.' The Sabbath was Saturday, not Sunday; why then do we keep Sunday holy instead of Saturday? The Church altered the observance of the Sabbath to the observance of Sunday in commemoration of our Lord having risen from the dead on Easter Sunday and of the Holy Ghost having descended upon the apostles on Whit Sunday. Protestants, who say that they go by the Bible and the Bible only and that they do not believe anything that is not in the Bible, must be rather puzzled by the keeping of Sunday when God distinctly said, 'Keep holy the Sabbath Day.' The word Sunday does not come anywhere in the Bible, so without knowing it, they are obeying the authority of the Catholic Church."[11]

We see then that the papacy is responsible for this change to God's laws and times and regards it as a mark of its authority. Other changes that have been brought into the Christian church by the papacy include the adoration of the Virgin, penance, the doctrines of purgatory and limbo, the doctrine of indulgences, and the adoration of images.

Thus far the papacy fulfils the requirements of the prophecy. What of the three and a half years which would mark the limits of its power? Just as God uses symbols in prophecy to heighten or to cloak the meaning, so God uses a time-scale in which one day stands for one year.

By comparing various usages of this scale, such as in the book of Revelation where periods of three and a half years, forty-two months and one thousand, two hundred and sixty days are treated as equal we can determine that the prophetic year consisted of 360 days, in common with the reckoning of those times and in particular the mathematics of Babylon.[12]

Is there some period of 1,260 years that is significant in the history of the papacy as a political power? In the year 533 AD the Byzantine Emperor Justinian issued a decree giving a large measure of political power to the officials of the Catholic church and in particular to the Bishop of Rome. His purpose was to subvert the Catholic faction in the occupied parts of the Roman empire, which he wanted to re-conquer.

In due course Justinian's general Belisarius defeated first the Vandals in North Africa and then the Ostrogoths in Italy. Rome itself fell to him late in 537 AD.

The office of Bishop of Rome was an office that offered labour, persecution and even martyrdom. The one thing it did not offer was power. In consequence, up until this time it had been held by a succession of godly men who, with only two exceptions, are called saints by the Catholic church.

With Belisarius in Rome, however, it was obvious that the Edict of Justinian could now be put into effect. The office of bishop of Rome now offered the dazzling prospect of political power in succession to the Caesars.

A renegade deacon named Vigilius moved swiftly to gain the confidence of the Empress Theodora and with her backing departed for Rome. Belisarius was reluctantly obliged to arrest the reigning pope, St. Silverius, and allow the installation of the usurper as Pope Vigilius. St Silverius was starved to death on the island of Palmaria in the Ligurian Sea just off Naples. He is venerated as a martyr and his feast day is June 20.

This sordid adventure took place in the year 537 AD but the new pope was not secure in his new found position. Rome was besieged by the Ostrogoths who had appointed Silverius and it was not until March, 538 AD that the Goths were finally defeated and driven away from Rome.

This victory marked the beginning of the political papacy. One thousand, two hundred and sixty years later, in February, 1798 AD, the French Revolutionary armies occupied the city of Rome and dethroned the reigning pope. Other popes had been

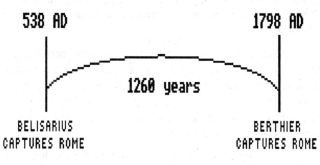

dethroned by military force but always in support of another claimant. This time there was no other claimant and the French revolutionaries intended no successor. When Pope Pius VI died in France there was an interregnum of seven months until the French realised that they needed someone to control the church and allowed the election of Pius VII.

The Concordat of 1801 between Pius VII and the Emperor Napoleon, however, stripped the papacy of its political power in France and set the precedent for other settlements that progressively restricted papal power until the papacy was left with the bare couple of acres of the Vatican City.[13]

If we accept that the papacy fulfils all the stipulations of the prophecy, we must also accept God's judgement on that institution.

"'As I looked thrones were set in place and the Ancient of Days took His seat. His clothing was as white as snow; the hair of His head was white like wool. His throne was flaming with fire and its wheels were all ablaze. A river of fire was flowing, coming out from before Him. Thousands upon thousands attended Him; ten thousand times ten thousand stood before Him. The court was seated and the books were opened.'" Daniel 7:9, 10

During the time that the heavenly court was in session the little horn continued its blasphemous career.

" 'Then I continued to watch because of the boastful words the horn was speaking. I kept looking until the beast was slain and its body destroyed and thrown into the blazing fire. (The other beasts had been stripped of their authority, but were allowed to live for a period of time.)' " Daniel 7:11, 12

Babylon, Persia and Greece had come upon the scene of history and for a brief period ruled the world. Their dominion came to an end, but they continued in existence as people or even as nations. Not so with the fourth beast and its offspring, the little horn. When its dominion ended it would be judged and destroyed.

Verse 26 makes it clear that the court sits after the 1,260 days have ended. There is therefore a period of unspecified length during which the papacy, though shorn of political power, continues its career of opposition to God and His law.

Again we see the fulfilment of the prophecy. Although the papacy has taken steps to reform itself, notably through the famous Vatican II council, none of its claims to spiritual authority have been abandoned. Far from yielding to the sovereignty of God, the papacy has proclaimed two dogmas - the Immaculate Conception and Papal Infallibility - that are not taught in Scripture and rest upon its own authority alone.

" 'In my vision at night I looked and there before me was one like a son of man coming with the clouds of heaven. He approached the Ancient of Days and was led into His presence. He was given authority, glory and sovereign power; all peoples, nations and men of every language worshipped Him. His dominion is an everlasting dominion that will not pass away and His kingdom is one that will never be destroyed.' " Daniel 7:13, 14

As a result of the court's decision a being like an ordinary human is led before God and is given total dominion, great glory and absolute sovereignty. Christians will recognise only One Who fulfils these requirements and that is the Lord Jesus Christ. At the second coming Jesus begins His reign as King of kings and Lord of lords.

It is interesting to notice that between the fall of the political papacy in 1798 and the second advent there is an unspecified period of time. On earth the papacy continues to blaspheme and in heaven God sits in judgement attended by the angelic hosts.

" ' "Then the sovereignty, power and greatness of the kingdoms under the whole heaven will be handed over to the saints, the people of the Most High." ' " Daniel 7:27

There will be those on earth who recognise the sovereignty of God alone and who reject the authority of the little horn. These keep God's laws and God's times and thus are fitted for a place in God's eternal kingdom when "the meek shall inherit the earth."

1. Older expositors identified the four heads as the four generals who divided Alexander's conquests between them. These were Ptolemy, Antiochus, Lysimachus and Cassander. In fact Antiochus was at first an adherant of Ptolemy and only later came to independent power. Lysimachus and Cassander quickly disappeared amid intrigues and battles, so I prefer the more enduring divisions that eventually appeared.

2. Daniel 7:8, 24

3. Daniel 7:25

4. Take for example the Reverend E. Hoare, Canon of Canterbury Cathedral. "In both prophecies" (Daniel chapters two and seven) "there is a description of four kingdoms which should in succession be supreme in political power and which should fill up an interval between Daniel and the Advent.

"1. There is the head of gold in Nebuchadnezzar's image, the same as the lion in the vision of Daniel.

"2. There is next the breast and arms of silver, corresponding to the bear of Daniel.

"3. After that the belly and thighs of brass, representing the same nation as the leopard of the prophet.

"4. And following them is the last kingdom of the four, represented to Nebuchadnezzar as the legs of iron and the feet part of iron and part of clay and to Daniel as a beast dreadful and terrible and strong exceedingly.

". . . Now the remarkable, and I believe I may say the indisputable, fact, is that, according to the prophecy all these four kingdoms have arisen. They have followed each other exactly as it was predicted. Babylon was the head of gold or the lion. The Medes and Persians were the breast of silver or the bear. Greece, always called 'the brazen armed' in classic poetry, was the belly and the thighs of brass or the leopard. And then the mighty power of Rome, far exceeding all the others in its terrible strength, with the legs of iron in the royal image and the teeth of iron in the prophetic beast. Thus far there is an agreement almost unanimous among the students of prophetic Scripture.

". . . I believe that the little horn diverse from all the rest is the Papal power, and that the time, times and dividing of a time, which is to be the limit of its power, stands in prophetic figure for 1260 years." Reverend E. Hoare, Rome, Turkey and Jerusalem, London: Chas. J. Thyne, 1914. pp.5-8, 13

5. If there are any who doubt this charitable assertion about the Muslims it is sufficient to consider how many churches were left functioning in Palestine after the Muslim conquest and how many mosques were left functioning in Spain after the Christian conquest. It is only in recent years that Christians have exceeded the toleration of Islam.

6. For example, Foxe's record of a group of Lollards burnt near Coventry. Their crime was that they taught their children the Lord's Prayer and the Creed in the English language.

7. Session 4 of the Fourth Lateran Council.

8. History of the English Church and People, Book 2 Chapter 2

9. Ecclesiastical History, Book 5 Chapter 22.

10. Ecclesiastical History, Book 7 Chapter 19

11. Canon Cafferata, The Catechism Simply Explained, London: Burns, Oates and Washbroune Ltd., 1947. p. 89

12. The Babylonians worked to a number base of 60 (the modern world uses the decimal system, a number base of 10). This is the reason why we have 360 degrees in a circle and sixty minutes in an hour.

13. It is noteworthy that as the political power of the papacy decreased, so its spiritual power has increased till today the whole world respects the sincerity of pontiffs such as John Paul II. On the contrary, when the papacy achieved political power in 538 AD the effect on the papacy was such that very few of the popes after that date have been regarded by the Roman Catholic church itself as worthy of the appellation "saint".

DANIEL

Chapter 8

By the third year of Belshazzar's reign the political scene had undergone a drastic change. Babylonian politicians had looked forward to a long-drawn out struggle between the Medes and the Persians which would only weaken both and make Babylon's eastern frontier more secure. Instead the defection of Harpaxes, Astyges' trusted general, resulted in the unification of Persia under a strong ruler whose ambitions would certainly be directed towards the fertile plains of Mesopotamia.

Overnight the eastern provinces, which at this time probably included the formerly independent kingdom of Elam, became important. Troop reinforcements, military inspectors and committees on defence poured into the neglected province. Among the important government officials crowding the decaying royal residence at Susa was the aging Daniel.

"'In the third year of King Belshazzar's reign, I, Daniel, had a vision, after the one that had already appeared to me. In my vision I saw myself in the citadel of Susa in the province of Elam; in the vision I was beside the Ulai Canal.'" Daniel 8:1, 2

No doubt Daniel had gone down to the river in search of cool breezes, shade and peace from the crowds in the narrow streets of the baking city above and the bustling, self-important courtiers in the citadel. As he relaxed beside the meandering, muddy stream his eye was caught by a movement over on the eastern bank.

"'I looked up and there before me was a ram with two horns, standing beside the canal, and the horns were long. One of the horns was longer than the other but grew up later.

I watched the ram as he charged towards the west and the north and the south. No animal could stand against him and none could rescue from his power. He did as he pleased and became great.'" Daniel 8:3, 4

When the symbolic part of the vision ended God provided an interpreter for Daniel and for us.

" 'While I, Daniel, was watching the vision and trying to understand it, there before me stood one who looked like a man. I heard a man's voice from the Ulai calling "Gabriel[1], tell this man the meaning of the vision."'

" 'As he came near the place where I was standing I was terrified and fell prostrate. "Son of man," he said to me, "understand that the vision concerns the time of the end."'

" 'While he was speaking to me I was in a deep sleep with my face to the ground. Then he touched me and raised me to my feet. He said: 'I am going to tell you what will happen later in the time of wrath, because the vision concerns the appointed time of the end. The two horned ram that you saw represents the kings of Media and Persia.'" Daniel 8:15-20

At the angel's approach Daniel was seized with a holy terror and collapsed to the ground where he remained until the angel strengthened him and helped him to his feet.

Gabriel told Daniel that the vision concerned the "time of the end". This phrase recurs in the book of Daniel and is obviously significant to our interpretation of the visions. All Daniel's visions end with God's kingdom established in place of earthly kingdoms and the saints of God ruling in peace. As Christians we understand that this refers to the second coming of Christ when the kingdoms of this world are abolished and God's kingdom is set up in their place.

Daniel himself no doubt interpreted this as the restoration of the Jews from exile, a view that seemed to be supported by the visions of Ezekiel, his fellow exile. He looked forward eagerly to the happy day when he could return to the scenes of his childhood, the Land of Promise, the beautiful hill of Zion. Because of this he reckoned the time periods with an eye to the end of Babylon's rule.

The ram stood for Media and Persia and its career depicted the victorious march of the Persian armies north to Asia Minor and the steppes of southern Russia, west to Babylon and Palestine and south to Egypt. For a while indeed nothing could stand before the Persian war machine. "He did as he pleased and became great."

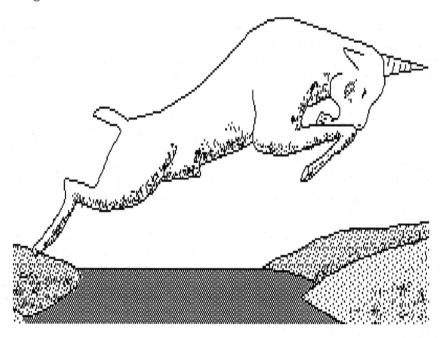

"'As I was thinking about this, suddenly a goat with a prominent horn between his eyes came from the west, crossing the whole earth without touching the ground. He came *towards the two-horned ram I had seen standing beside the canal and charged at him in great rage. I saw him attack the ram furiously, striking the ram and shattering his two horns. The ram was powerless to stand against him; the goat knocked him to the ground and trampled on him and none could rescue the ram from his power. The goat became very great but at the height of his power his large horn was broken off and in its place four prominent horns grew up towards the four winds of heaven.'" Daniel 8:5-8*

Again the symbol was interpreted to Daniel:

"'"The shaggy goat is the king of Greece and the large horn between his eyes is the first king. The four horns that replaced the one that was broken off represent four kingdoms that will emerge from his nation but will not have the same power.'" Daniel 8:20-22

Fighting goats were bred by wild hill tribes. When young their horns were twisted together to form a single, forward-pointing horn. One of these fighting goats appeared from the west, charging towards the dominant ram. At the first onset the ram's horns were smashed and after that the goat did as it pleased until it stood triumphant over the prostrate body of its rival. In the course of the fight, however, its single horn had been weakened and now broke. From the damaged roots sprouted four weak horns, twisting out in all directions.

A more dramatic and accurate picture of the fall of the Persian empire can hardly be imagined. Alexander launched his first attack in 334 BC with the crossing of the Granicus river. The decisive battle of Gaugamela took place three years later and by 327 BC Alexander was in India, the furthest extent of his conquests.

Four years later Alexander was dead and his vast empire was divided into four. The first division was between four of his generals - Ptolemy, Seleucus, Lysimachus and and Cassander. Subsequent civil wars produced a re-arrangement of the pieces, but still four divisions - the Ptolemies in Egypt, the Seleucids in Syria and Mesopotamia, the Antigonids in Greece itself and the city state of Pergamum in Asia Minor. The highlands of Persia were quietly abandoned to anarchy until the Parthians took over.

"'Out of one of them came another horn which started small but grew in power to the south and to the east and towards the Beautiful Land. It grew until it reached the host of the heavens and it threw some of the starry host down to the earth and trampled on them. It set itself up to be as great as the Prince of the host; it took away the daily sacrifice from him and the place of his sanctuary was brought low. Because of rebellion the host (armies) and the daily sacrifice were given over to it. It prospered in everything it did and truth was thrown to the ground.'" Daniel 8:9-12

In the interpretation of the dream Gabriel added the following details:

"'"In the latter part of their reign, when rebels have become completely wicked, a stern-faced king, a master of intrigue, will arise. He will become very strong but not by his own power. He will cause astounding devastation and will succeed in whatever he does. He will destroy the mighty men and the holy people. He will cause deceit to prosper and he will consider himself superior. When they feel secure, he will destroy many and take his stand against the Prince of princes. Yet he will be destroyed, but not by human power."'" Daniel 8:23-25*

The description of this third power begins with an ambiguity. In Hebrew the word "horn" is feminine while the word "wind" may be either masculine or feminine. Verse 9 uses a feminine "one", suggesting that the little horn came from one of the four previous horns. On the other hand the word "them" is masculine, referring to "wind". As "wind" may be either feminine or masculine it is probably better to assume that the little horn sprouted from one of the four winds of heaven, for this allows both "one" and "them" to refer to the same noun.

The vision and the interpretation supplied by Gabriel describes the Roman empire[2] which became strong as much by clever diplomacy as by armed force, which did indeed destroy the Jewish state and under whose rule the "Prince of princes" was crucified. Rome expanded south to Egypt, east to Greece and Asia Minor as well as to the Pleasant Land.

There are, however, other details that do not fit with the history of Rome. The Roman armies never entered into battle against the armies of heaven and certainly never "threw some of the starry host to the earth." When Rome's empire finally ceased, it was destroyed by human hands - the barbarians who repeatedly sacked the Eternal City. Yet the prophecy says "He will be destroyed, but not by human power."

Some continue the prophecy to include the Roman Catholic church and the papacy, which would certainly fit the prediction "It set itself up to be as great as the Prince of the host" and certainly can be accused of having "thrown truth to the ground". Yet only in the most metaphorical of ways could the papacy be said to have cast down the armies of heaven.

The solution is to be found in the twelfth chapter of the book of Revelation. Here another power is introduced that, like the little horn of Daniel, has similarities to both pagan and papal Rome and yet is more than both.

"Then another sign appeared in heaven: an enormous red dragon with seven heads and ten horns and seven crowns on his heads. His tail swept a third of the stars out of the sky and flung them to the earth." Revelation 12:3, 4

Later in John's vision this mysterious power is clearly identified.

"And there was war in heaven. Michael and his angels fought against the dragon and the dragon and his angels fought back but he was not strong enough and they lost their place in heaven. The great dragon was hurled down - that ancient serpent called the devil or Satan, who leads the whole world astray - he was hurled to the earth and his angels with him." Revelation 12:7-9

Satan is the power represented by the little horn; Satan working through his human agents of pagan as well as papal Rome, to oppress and persecute the people of God and to do away with the true worship of God. The prophecy declares that Satan will do away with the "daily" (the word sacrifice is implied) - the worship ordained by God - and "truth was thrown to the ground." Yet though the devil appears to prosper in everything he attempts, the assurance is given that he will be destroyed, though not by human power.

" 'Then I heard a holy one speaking and another holy one said to him, "How long will it take for the vision to be fulfilled - the vision concerning the daily sacrifice, the rebellion that causes desolation and the surrender of the sanctuary and of the host that will be trampled underfoot?" '

" 'He said to me, "It will take 2,300 evenings and mornings; then the sanctuary will be reconsecrated[3]." ' " Daniel 8:13, 14

At once Daniel's thoughts flew to the sanctuary in Jerusalem, lying in ruins ever since its destruction by Nebuzaradan 36 years before. Two thousand three hundred evenings and mornings. Quickly Daniel worked it out in his head. Just over six years! Better still, if the evenings and mornings were to be taken separately, making 1150 complete days, then the prediction covered a little more than three years!

How Daniel's mind raced as he pictured the fall of the oppressor, the glorious deliverance, the journey home and the arrival in the city of his youth. Then Gabriel shattered all his dreams.

" ' "The vision of the evenings and mornings that has been given you is true, but seal up the vision, for it concerns the distant future." ' " Daniel 8:26

Daniel doubtless knew of the year/day time-scale[4] and at Gabriel's words his heart sank. Two thousand three hundred years? The distant future? The shock of disappointment was more than he could bear.

" 'I, Daniel, was exhausted and lay ill for several days. Then I got up and went about the king's business. I was appalled by the vision; it was beyond understanding.' " Daniel 8:27

Abruptly the vision ended as the prophet's mind became incapable of receiving further information. Sick at heart, Daniel dragged himself back to his rooms and lay ill for several days before he was able to resume the important work for which he had come to Elam. He simply could not understand why the merciful God he served should decide to so prolong the captivity.

Of one thing he was certain: he himself would never see Jerusalem again.

---

1. This is the first mention in Scripture of the archangel Gabriel, whom we must assume to be the same as the archangel who appeared to Zachariah and to Mary. He appears in the next two visions as well.

2. Various commentators have attempted to identify the little horn of chapter 8 as Antiochus IV of the Seleucid empire. See the appendix to this chapter for the reasons why this identification is not acceptable.

3. The word "reconsecrated" is an unusual form of a common Hebrew verb meaning "to be just or righteous". This particular form only occurs this once in Scripture and so its exact shade of meaning is uncertain. Various suggestions have been made but the English term "to be vindicated" is perhaps the best summary of these suggestions.

4. Just as God used symbols in these visions, so He used a time scale by which a day in the prophecy stood for a calendar year. This is explicitly stated in Ezekiel 4:6. According to Babylonian science there were 360 days in a year and this is the figure that we should use when attempting to interpret the visions.

Appendix to Chapter 8

A superficial reading of chapter eight might seem to support the indentification of the little horn as Antiochus IV, for Antiochus "grew" out of one of the four horns and certainly persecuted the Jews and defiled the sanctuary. We have already indicated that the little horn came out of one of the winds rather than out of one of the horns. This, however, is the least of the objections to the Antiochus IV theory.

Antiochus IV was the son of Antiochus III, known as "the Great". For fourteen years he was held as a hostage in Rome following his father's defeat by the Romans. On coming to the throne he attempted to imitate his father's exploits by conquering the rival Ptolemies in Egypt but was ordered out of the country by an unarmed Roman senator, Gaius Popillius Laenas.

In an attempt to unify and strengthen his kingdom Antiochus fostered a policy of Hellenisation, and supported Jewish elements who wanted to bring in Greek ideas and practices. When the orthodox Jews rebelled Antiochus captured Jerusalem and converted the temple into a shrine of Zeus Olympios.

This blasphemy sparked off the Maccabean revolt which won independence for the Jews, despite Antiochus' army of 46,000 infantry, 8,500 cavalry and 306 armoured elephants. Desperate for money to support this huge army, Antiochus looted the temple of Nanaia in southern Iran. Not long afterwards he died at Isfahan and his death was widely regarded as a divine punishment for his sacrilege. Many people privately turned his cognomen of Epiphanes ("god manifest") into Epimanes ("lunatic").

This unstable king, who provoked his subjects into revolt, relied upon his huge army and died after robbing one of his own temples, can hardly fit the descriptions of the prophecy: "Prospered in everything it did . . . will become strong but not by his own power . . . master of intrigue . . . will succeed in whatever he does."

Perhaps most important of all, Antiochus, who died in 164 BC, cannot be said to have opposed the "Prince of princes".

There is one final convincing point against this identification. According to the prophecy it would be 2,300 days until the sanctuary was re-consecrated or vindicated. This makes six years and four months, and even if one adopts the suggestion that 1,150 complete days are meant, it still comes to three years and two months.

The historical records of the Maccabean revolt are quite definite about the length of time that the temple was desecrated.

"Now it so fell out that these things were done on the very same day on which their divine worship had fallen off and was reduced to a profane and common use, after three years time; for so it was that the temple was made desolate by Antiochus and so continued for three years. This desolation happened to the temple in the hundred forty and fifth year, on the twenty-fifth day of the month Appelleus and on the hundred and fifty-third Olympiad; but it was dedicated anew on the same day, the twenty-fifth of the month Appelleus, in the hundred and forty-eighth year and on the hundred and fifty-fourth Olympiad."[1]

"Now the fifteenth day of the month Casleu, in the hundred forty and fifth year, they set up the abomination of desolation upon the altar and builded idol altars throughout the cities of Judah on every side. . . . Now the five and twentieth day of the month they did sacrifice upon the idol altar which was upon the altar of God."[2]

"Now on the five and twentieth day of the ninth month, which is called the month Casleu, in the hundred forty and eighth year, they rose up betimes in the morning and offered sacrifice according to the law upon the new altar of burnt offerings which they had made. At what time and day the heathen had profaned it, even in that was it dedicated with songs and citherns and harps and cymbals."[3]

"Now upon the same day that the strangers profaned the temple, on the very same day it was cleansed again, even the five and twentieth day of the same month, which is Casleu."[4]

These three sources emphasise the fact that the temple was cleansed on exactly the same day of the same month as it was desecrated. There is no room here for two or four months beyond the span of three years. Unless, therefore we are willing to say that the God of heaven is unable to foretell the future accurately, we must conclude that Antiochus Ephiphanes cannot in any way be the fulfilment of the prophecy of Daniel chapter eight.

---

1. Josephus, Antiquities of the Jews, Book 12, Chapter VII, Section 6

2. 1 Maccabees 1:54, 59

3. 1 Maccabees 4:52-54

4. 2 Maccabees 10:5

DANIEL

Chapter 9

For eleven years, while Cyrus conquered Media, added Lydia to his empire and mustered his forces for the assault on Babylon, the hopes of the Jews in captivity rose steadily higher. Surely, they thought, this must be the Cyrus promised by the prophet Isaiah.

Daniel alone failed to share the general sense of hope and expectation. The words of the angel rang in his ears: "Seal up the vision, for it concerns the distant future." How could this Cyrus be the deliverer if the temple was not to be restored till the far-distant future?

In 539 BC Cyrus "took the hand of Marduk" in the age old ceremony by which a new king was introduced to the gods of Babylon; but instead of ruling in Babylon himself, Cyrus, who needed to be back in Persia, appointed Darius, a trusted Mede, to govern Babylonia. When Cyrus left without making any decree concerning the Jews Daniel's worst fears were realised and he sank into dark despair.

About this time someone showed Daniel a copy of the writings of Jeremiah. Daniel could still remember the stern face of the prophet and possibly had even heard him preach. Jeremiah's book, however, was written after Daniel and his friends were taken to Babylon as hostages and so was new to Daniel.

"'In the first year of Darius son of Xerxes, (a Mede by descent), who was made ruler over the Babylonian kingdom - in the first year of his reign, I, Daniel, understood from the Scriptures according to the word of the Lord given to Jeremiah the prophet, that the desolations of Jerusalem would last seventy years.'" Daniel 9:1, 2

As he eagerly read through the book Daniel's eye was caught by a prediction made in the very year that he and his friends were carried to Babylon.

"Therefore the Lord Almighty says this: 'Because you have not listened to My words I will summon all the peoples of the north and My servant Nebuchadnezzar, king of Babylon,' declares the Lord, 'and I will bring them against this land and its inhabitants and against all the surrounding nations. I will completely destroy them and make them an object of horror and scorn and an everlasting ruin. I will banish from them the sounds of joy and gladness, the voices of bride and bridegroom, the sound of millstones and the light of the lamp. This whole country will become a desolate wasteland and these nations will serve the king of Babylon for seventy years.'

"'But when the seventy years are fulfilled, I will punish the king of Babylon and his nation, the land of the Babylonians, for their guilt.' declares the Lord." Jeremiah 25:8-12

Daniel counted up the reigns of the kings of Babylon and discovered that sixty-six years had passed since he and his friends had seen Jerusalem for the last time.[1] Surely their captivity must be drawing to a close! Surely this Cyrus must be the predicted deliverer!

Yet the angel had specifically informed him that the temple would not be "vindicated" until a point two thousand three hundred years in the future. Why?

Daniel turned back to the book and a little further on he found a clue. It was in the copy of a letter Jeremiah sent to the captives in Babylon eight or nine years after Daniel was taken captive.

"This is what the Lord says: 'When seventy years are completed for Babylon, I will come to you and fulfil My gracious promise to bring you back to this place. For I know the plans I have for you,' declares the Lord, 'plans to prosper you and not to harm you, plans to give you hope and a future. Then you will call upon Me and come and pray to Me, and I will listen to you. You will seek Me and find Me when you seek Me with all your heart. I will be found by you,' declares the Lord, 'and will bring you back from captivity.'" Jeremiah 29:10-14

"With all your heart." The words burned in Daniel's mind. "You will seek Me and find Me" but only "when you seek Me with all your heart." As he looked around him Daniel was aware that his people were very far from seeking the Lord with all their hearts. So many had settled down in comfort, building up prosperous businesses and contracting advantageous marriages with the heathen around them.

Daniel determined that he at least would seek the Lord with all his heart.

"'I turned to the Lord God and pleaded with Him in prayer and petition, in fasting and in sackcloth and ashes. I prayed to the Lord my God and confessed.'" Daniel 9:3, 4

In an agony of mind and spirit Daniel opened his heart to God, acknowledging that his people had sinned in the past and were still sinning against God, despite the judgements that had come upon them. Then he turned to the real purpose of his prayer.

"'Now, our God, hear the prayers and petitions of your servant. For Your sake, O Lord, look with favour on Your desolate sanctuary. Give ear, O God, and hear; open Your eyes and see the desolation of the city that bears Your Name. We do not make requests of You because we are righteous but because of Your great mercy. O Lord, listen! O Lord, forgive! O Lord, hear and act! For Your sake, O my God, do not delay, because Your city and Your people bear Your Name.'" Daniel 9:17-19

A footstep or a touch on his arm, caused Daniel to open his eyes. A man stood by him, a man whom he recognised.

"'While I was still in prayer Gabriel, the man I had seen in the earlier vision, came to me in swift flight about the time of the evening sacrifice.'" Daniel 9:21

The vision that had been abruptly terminated by Daniel's collapse so long before was to be continued as if the intervening years had never been. Gabriel's explanation carried on at the exact point that it had been broken off.

"'"Seventy sevens (weeks) are decreed for your people and your holy city to finish transgression, to put an end to sin, to atone for wickedness, to bring in everlasting righteousness, to seal up vision and prophecy and to anoint the Most Holy."'" Daniel 9:24

The Hebrew word translated as "decreed" literally means "to cut" or "to cut off". While the vision of chapter 8 extended into the distant future, a shorter period of 490 years was to be "cut off" for the Jews and for Jerusalem. The purpose of this period was to atone for wickedness, to seal up (or validate) the vision and the prophecy and to anoint the Most Holy.

Although the text does not specify whether it is a Most Holy place or a Most Holy person that is to be anointed, the following verse speaks of an Anointed One, a ruler, so we are justified in accepting that the purpose of this period was to bring about the anointing of the Most Holy One, the Anointed ruler, the Messiah.

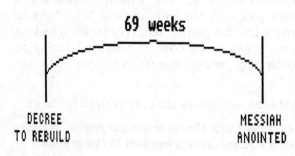

69 weeks

DECREE
TO REBUILD

MESSIAH
ANOINTED

"'"Know and understand this: From the issuing of the decree to restore and rebuild Jerusalem until the Anointed One, the Ruler, comes, there will be seven 'sevens' and sixty-two 'sevens'. It will be rebuilt with streets and a trench, but in times of trouble."'" Daniel 9:25

The Hebrew word translated as "Anointed One" is literally "Messiah", but kings or priests could be called "anointed ones" as when David declined to harm "the Lord's anointed."[2] Here however we have an "Anointed One" whose coming will "seal up vision and prophecy", "finish transgression" and "bring in everlasting righteousness." This must surely be the Messiah, the promised Redeemer of Israel.

By these words Gabriel reveals to Daniel the date of the Messiah's anointing and thus of the dawn of the Messianic age. It will come sixty-nine 'sevens' after a decree is issued to restore and rebuild Jerusalem. Then Gabriel let Daniel in on a terrible secret.

"'"After the sixty-two 'sevens' the Anointed One will be cut off and will have nothing. The people of the ruler who will come will destroy the city and the sanctuary. The end will come like a flood: war will continue until the end and desolations have been decreed. He will confirm a covenant with many for one 'seven'. In the middle of the 'seven' he will put an end to sacrifice and offering. On a wing (of the temple) he will set up an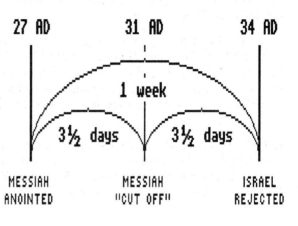
abomination that causes desolation, until the end that is decreed is poured out on him."'" Daniel 9:26, 27

Instead of ruling in triumph, the Messiah will be "cut off", a phrase that implies execution with overtones of Divine displeasure rather than natural death. Furthermore both city and sanctuary will be destroyed again and war will continue till the end - the end of the longer period. During the final 'seven' of the seventy a covenant will be confirmed but half-way through that period the sacrifices and offerings will be terminated.

The traditional interpretation of this prophecy focuses on the Messiah. By counting the number of Passover feasts mentioned in the Gospels we conclude that Jesus had a public ministry after His baptism of approximately three and a half years. At the end of that time He was executed - "cut off" - and at His death the veil of the temple was ripped from top to bottom,[3] thus indicating that as far as God was concerned the temple rituals were at an end.

It was the Romans who destroyed Jerusalem and the temple. This interpretation is supported by Jesus Himself Who identified the Roman armies of 70 AD with the "abomination that causes desolation".[4]According to Eusebius[5] the early Christians in Judea heeded this warning and although a million Jews perished in the siege of Jerusalem not a single Christian lost his life.

The question is, when does this period of seventy 'sevens' or 490 years begin? According to the prophecy it commences at "the issuing of the decree to restore and rebuild Jerusalem."

The Bible mentions three separate decrees concerning Jerusalem: the first is the original decree of Cyrus, given in his first year (probably 537/536 BC) which is recorded in Ezra 1:1-4. An undated decree of Darius (but falling about his second year, 520/519 BC) which is found in Ezra 6:1-12 merely reconfirms the decree of Cyrus.

The third decree is the one given to Ezra himself and its terms are laid out in Ezra 7:12-26 The most important part of this decree is the last part, granting to Ezra and his successors the right to administer their own law, enforced by punishment up to and including the death penalty. In effect this decree grants autonomy to the Jewish province of the Persian empire.

"And you, Ezra, in accordance with the wisdom of your God, which you possess, appoint magistrates and judges to administer justice to all the people of Trans-Euphrates - all who know the laws of your God. And you are to teach any who do not know them. Whoever does not obey the law of your God and the law of the king must surely be punished by death, banishment, confiscation of property or imprisonment." Ezra 7:25, 26

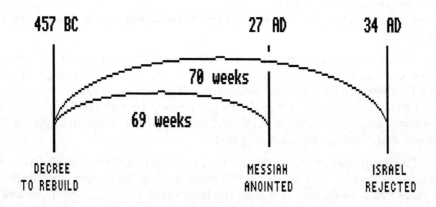

This decree is dated to the seventh year of Artaxerxes, which was the year 457 BC.[6] The sixty-nine "sevens" or 483 years that lead up to the anointing of the Messiah bring us to the year 27 AD.[7] We should look for some event in that year that would mark the anointing of the Messiah.

Matthew, Mark and John are all silent upon the chronology of the life of Christ, so we are very fortunate indeed that Luke, a Greek, also wrote a biography of Jesus. We are less fortunate in that Luke used the reigns of Roman emperors as his means of dating events instead of the old fashioned Olympiads, which would have given us a more secure chronology.

"In the fifteenth year of the reign of Tiberius Caesar - when Pontius Pilate was governor of Judea, Herod tetrarch of Galilee, his brother Philip tetrarch of Iturea and Traconitis, and Lysanias tetrarch of Abilene - during the high priesthood of Annas and Caiaphas, the word of God came to John son of Zechariah in the desert." Luke 3:1, 2

The various tetrarchies and high priesthoods mentioned by Luke fall within the period 26-34 AD so that our attention must focus on the fifteenth year of Tiberius. Augustus, Tiberius' predecessor, died on August 19 in the year 14 AD. The Talmud[8] declares that the Jews calculated the years of Gentile kings from autumn to autumn which means that Augustus' first year spanned the short period from August 19 to mid-October of 14 AD.[9]

On this basis we can say that the fifteenth year of Tiberius was the year 27/28 AD which is four hundred and eighty three years after the decree of Artaxerxes in the year 457 BC. Thus Jesus was baptised and anointed by the Holy Ghost in the shape of a dove in the autumn of 27 AD, in exact fulfilment of the prophecy.

There remained yet one week set apart for the Jews. During half of that week Jesus the Messiah travelled through Israel teaching the people and healing the sick. At the end of three and a half years (as best as we can tell) he was "cut off", crucified as a common criminal.

"He will have nothing." The King James translation renders this phrase as "but not for Himself", that is to say, the death will be neither for His own faults nor for His own benefit. As Isaiah had predicted, the suffering servant "was cut off from the land of the living; for the transgression of my people he was stricken."[10]

When the veil of the temple was torn by unseen hands as Jesus cried "It is finished!" God declared that now the way into the holiest was open, with no more need for sacrifices or a human priestly ministry. Thus the Messiah "put an end to sacrifice and offering" and became Himself the great High Priest of the New Covenant.

After Messiah's death, however, there was yet the second half of the final week. Although His people had rejected His Son, God did not yet reject them and Jesus Himself commanded His disciples to begin their preaching in Jerusalem and Judea. Only when the Jews showed by persecuting His followers that Jesus' sacrifice had failed to touch their hearts did God finally turn from His people.

"'"The people of the ruler who will come will destroy the city and the sanctuary."'"
Daniel 9:26

Out of respect for its beauty Titus forbade his soldiers to destroy or damage the temple. During the frenzy of the fighting, however, a soldier threw a firebrand and within minutes the temple was ablaze. Despite the best efforts of Titus and his entourage to extinguish the flames the sanctuary was totally destroyed.

"'"The end will come like a flood: war will continue until the end and desolations have been decreed."'" Daniel 9:26

After their final rejection by God the nation lingered on in anarchy and chaos, crushed by Titus in 70 AD only to rise again in 132 AD and follow Bar Kosiba, whom Rabbi Akiba hailed as Bar Kokhba, the Son of the Star, in allusion to Balaam's famous Messianic prophecy. Here was a messiah after their own hearts and the whole nation responded to his call and revolted against the Romans.

Once more the legions marched through Judea and encamped around Jerusalem. This time there was to be no return. Hadrian destroyed the city, scattered the materials that had been gathered for the rebuilding of the temple, and on its site erected a pagan temple. Jews were forbidden to come within sight of the city.

"'"On a wing of the temple he will set up an abomination that causes desolation until the end that is decreed is poured out on him."'" Daniel 9:27

Later rulers relaxed the total ban on Jewish inhabitants of Jerusalem but for most of the intervening centuries the number of Jews in Jerusalem remained very small indeed, an oppressed minority in a land of enemies. Not until the early nineteenth century was there renewed interest in immigration to Israel aided by the efforts of philanthropists such as Sir Moses Montifiore.

The situation began to change from the mid-1840's onwards. New Jewish quarters were built around Jerusalem, there was increased immigration into Palestine and the Jewish life in Palestine became more open, bold and vigorous. This change in attitude led, eventually, to the modern State of Israel. As we shall see in the next chapter, the mid-1840's have a particular prophetic significance.

---

1. According to the best chronology available, Nebuchadnezzar captured Jerusalem and took Daniel hostage in the year 605 BC. Cyrus entered Babylon late in 539 BC, which some have taken as his first year. However we should realise that according to the "accession year" principle, the first year of the monarch would not begin until the following spring, therefore Cyrus' first regnal year is the year 538/537 BC.

The Bible gives us the additional information that Darius ruled in Babylon for at least one year - the year 538/537 BC. The very earliest that Cyrus could be said to be king of Babylon would be the year 537/536 BC, but if Darius lived into that year, then Cyrus' first year as king of Babylon would be the year 536/535 BC. Even if we take the earlier year, however, this would make seventy years by inclusive reckoning, a form of calculation well understood and much used in Bible times. (For example: the three days that Jesus spent in the tomb, Friday to Sunday, must be reckoned inclusively.)

2. 1 Samuel 26:11

3. Matthew 27:51

4. *"So when you see standing in the holy place 'the abomination that causes desolation' spoken of through the prophet Daniel - let the reader understand - then let those who are in Judea flee to the mountains."* Matthew 24:15, 16

A popular interpretation of the present day divides the final 'seven' from the preceding sixty-nine, placing it at the end of time. It is difficult to justify this. Why is a similar gap not put between the seven and the sixty-two 'sevens'? Furthermore this modern view ignores the identification Jesus made of the "abomination that causes desolation", instead bringing in a strange Antichrist whose career is described in great (and usually fanciful) detail.

5. Eusebius, Ecclesiastical History, book 3 chapter 5.3

6. A number of uncertainties attach to this dating. For example: we cannot even be sure which Artaxerxes is referred to! It is generally accepted, however, that Ezra's benefactor was Artaxerxes Longimanus, who reigned from 465-423 BC.

A second uncertainty concerns the precise indentification of his seventh year. According to Persian spring to spring chronology the seventh year of Artaxerxes Longimanus would be the year 458 BC. The Elephantine papyrii show that Jews were accustomed to using their own autumn to autumn chronology. Assuming that Ezra followed this custom, the seventh year of Artaxerxes should be put in 457 BC.

7. When a calculation crosses the BC/AD divide one must always add a year. This is because there is no year zero, but 1 BC is immediately followed by 1 AD. For example, from mid-way through 2 BC to mid-way through 2 AD is only three years, not four as one might have expected.

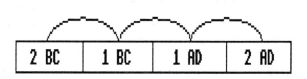

8. Mishnah: Rosh Hashanah

9. The way in which Josephus counts the years of Herod the Great's reign provides evidence that by this time the Jews used the non-accession year method of counting. That is, at the New Year's Day following his accession to the throne a ruler began the second year of his reign. It is therefore likely that they used the same method in reckoning the years of Tiberius' reign.

10. Isaiah 53:8

DANIEL

The 2,300 Days

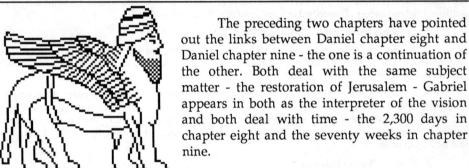

The preceding two chapters have pointed out the links between Daniel chapter eight and Daniel chapter nine - the one is a continuation of the other. Both deal with the same subject matter - the restoration of Jerusalem - Gabriel appears in both as the interpreter of the vision and both deal with time - the 2,300 days in chapter eight and the seventy weeks in chapter nine.

The use of the word "cut off" in chapter nine indicates that the seventy weeks are but part of a longer period and it is obvious that this must be the period of time mentioned in the interrupted vision of chapter eight. The only question remaining is: are the seventy weeks cut off from the beginning or the end of the longer period?

The answer is found in the phrase "abomination that causes desolation" which follows the conclusion of the seventy weeks of chapter 9. Daniel 8:13 mentions the "rebellion that causes desolation" which destroys the sanctuary and which endures for 2,300 days or years. As the "abomination that causes desolation" which is part of the 2,300 days comes after the seventy weeks it follows that the seventy weeks form the first part of the 2,300 days.

In chapter eight Daniel is given no starting point for the time period and we may assume that his weakness terminated the vision before this information could be given. However, if our conclusion is correct and the two visions are related, it follows that both time periods have the same starting point - the decree for the restoration of Jerusalem.

This decree, we have already seen, was given in the year 457 BC. Simple arithmetic will tell us that the 2,300 years of the prophecy bring us to the year 1843/1844 AD. What is the event which is supposed to mark the termination of the prophecy? What should have happened in 1843/1844?

In many ways the 1840's were a significant time in this planet's history. In politics there was the Year of Revolutions in 1848 when France, Italy, Germany, the Austro-Hungarian Empire, Switzerland and even Turkey underwent traumatic changes in government.

More significantly from the point of view of the struggle between God and Satan for men's souls, the Communist Manifesto was published in London by Karl Marx and Friedrich Engels in 1848. This was the start of one of the most openly anti-religious movements the world has ever seen, with phrases like "the opium of the people" characterising the movement's attitude to Christianity and religion.

In the scientific field, in 1842 a little known vicar's son named Charles Darwin developed a theory to explain the origin of species although he did not publish his famous book for seventeen years. Darwin did not intend to attack religion by his theory, yet the theory of evolution became one of the most significant causes in the decline of religion.

In the spiritual field the 1840's saw a burst of new religions arising, many of them in the New World. Mormonism was founded by Joseph Smith who claimed to base his religion on divinely revealed golden plates. Christian Science sprang from the teachings of Mary Baker Eddy and away over in Persia Bahai-Ullah founded the Bahai faith. Modern spiritualism, the claimed ability to contact the dead, began with the Fox sisters in 1844.

These all undermined the Bible's position and authority by presenting alternative sources of authority - the Book of Mormon, the revelations of the spirits or the wisdom of the East. In addition they presented counterfeit manifestations of the Biblical gifts of the Spirit which devalued the genuine gift of prophecy.

At the same time in nearly every Christian country there was a sudden upsurge of interest in the prophecies of the Biblical books of Daniel and Revelation. As a result of their studies many preachers proclaimed that Christ would return in the 1840's; some were even more explicit and fixed on 1843 or 1844.

One of the most colourful of these preachers was the converted Jew Joseph Wolff who travelled, at risk of his life, all through the Muslim countries of Asia and the Middle East, preaching that Jesus was the Messiah and that He was coming back in 1847. This occasioned him considerable embarrassment when he paid a return visit to Bokhara after the expected date. The Emir taxed him with the failure of his prediction but no exact record remains of Wolff's reply!

Another was Edward Irving, a popular Presbyterian preacher in London, who established his own denomination - the Catholic Apostolic Church. The emphasis of this church was on the nearness of the Second Coming, even when the predicted date in the mid-1840's passed. Irving became involved with charismatic tongues speaking and was advised through this "gift" to appoint twelve apostles. No provision was made for replacing the original twelve and the last died some time in the 1950's, after which the Catholic Apostolic Church became extinct.

Perhaps the most unexpected was Manuel de Lacunza, a Jesuit from Chile who wrote "La Venida del Mesias en Gloria y Magestad", a book which was not published until after his death. Although he wrote under the pen name of a Jewish rabbi, the author's identity was soon known, but that did not prevent the book being placed on the Index of Prohibited Books n 1824.

The most successful of the preachers who proclaimed the Second Advent in the mid-1840's was William Miller, an American farmer and Bapist lay-preacher. Through personal Bible study he became convinced, on the basis of Daniel 8:14, that Jesus would return in 1843/1844. He gained thousands of followers who quietly prepared for the expected End of the World and who were bitterly disappointed when the appointed day passed and nothing happened.

Between them these men - and many others less colourful - awakened Christians to the wonderful truth of the Second Coming, the blessed hope, which had for many become a forgotten doctrine. Various conferences were held; in Britain Edward Irving and others organised the Albury Conferences for the study of prophecy. In America the Millerites organised a series of meetings in different places for the same purpose.

Naturally the Millerites concerned themselves with a more specific question: What was the real significance of 1844? They concentrated on the verses which had given them the date - Daniel 8:13, 14

"'Then I heard a holy one speaking and another holy one said to him, "How long will it take for the vision to be fulfilled - the vision concerning the daily sacrifice, the rebellion that causes desolation and the surrender of the sanctuary and of the host that will be trampled underfoot?"'

"'He said to me, "It will take 2,300 evenings and mornings; then the sanctuary will be reconsecrated."'"

The first thing they noted was that the passage concerned the sanctuary, the Jewish temple, and its sacrifices. If, as they concluded, the time period extended down to 1844 and did not refer to Antiochus Epiphanes, then they were faced with the fact that there was no Jewish temple in 1844!

The solution lay in the book of Hebrews in the New Testament.

"The point of what we are saying it this: We do have such a high priest who sat down at the right hand of the throne of the Majesty in heaven and who serves in the sanctuary, the true tabernacle set up by the Lord, not by man." Hebrews 8:1, 2

Christians under the New Covenant do not worship in an earthly temple nor are they served by an earthly priesthood. Instead they focus on Jesus Christ, priest after the order of Melchizedek, who ministers in the only valid temple - the temple in heaven.

This conclusion led them to study the temple and its services. They found that there were seven great festivals or "sabbaths" each year when the Jews worshipped God in the temple. In these "sabbaths" they discovered the whole of the Christian era.

According the Leviticus 23, the first festival of the year was the Passover in the first month. For the Jews this event celebrated their deliverance from Egypt but Christians see in it a deeper significance. It was at Passover time that Jesus died and his blood delivers from the more awful bondage of sin and death. The Christian era begins with the death of Christ.

The second festival was a feast of firstfruits when a sheaf of the first grain harvested in the land was brought to the temple and presented to God. Matthew 2752 tells us that at Jesus' resurrection a number of "saints" were also raised and Ephesians 4:8 indicates that when Jesus returned to heaven He took with Him a number of captives - the firstfruits of the great harvest of the earth.

The third festival came fifty days after the second. In Greek this is the word 'pente', for which reason the feast is known as Pentecost. During this feast the fruit of the completed harvest was presented to God. At Pentecost the Holy Spirit was poured out on mankind and the great work of proclaiming the Lordship of Jesus Christ was begun, a work which will continue right up until the Second Coming.

The fourth festival did not occur until the seventh month when the rigours of summer were past and the autumn work about to begin. On the first day of this month priests blew the 'shofar' on every street corner in the land to warn people that the most solemn day of the year was approaching - the Day of Atonement, the Day of Judgement.

The fifth festival followed just ten days laer and unlike all the other religious occasions, which were times of feasting and rejoicing, the Day of Atonement was a time of fasting and self-denial. Jewish tradition teaches that on this day the fate of every individual is fixed for the coming year.

The final festival, which incorporated two of the "sabbaths" was the Feast of Tabernacles when the whole nation went camping, leaving their houses to live in rough shelters for a whole week. The children must have loved it! It was a reminder of the wanderings in the wilderness and celebrated the fact that those wanderings were now over and the people safe in Canaan. To us it symbolises the end of our pilgrimage in this world and our entrance into the heavenly Canaan.

We see then that the death of Jesus, the work of the church and the final reward of the saints are all pre-figured by the festivals of the Jewish year. What are we to make of the Day of Atonement which comes towards the end of the festival cycle and therefore in symbol towards the end of the Christian era?

The first thing to notice is that unlike all the other festivals the Day of Atonement was a time of fasting not feasting, of self-denial instead of rejoicing. Yom Kippur is still regarded by religious Jews as a time of awe and fear. Even the non-religious tend to visit the synagogue on this day.

The second point is that the Day of Atonement had very little to do with the people. The description of the ritual given in Leviticus 16 makes it plain that the services of the Day of Atonement were exclusively to do with the sanctuary itself.

"In this way he will make atonement for the Most Holy Place because of the uncleanness and rebellion of the Israelites, whatever their sins have been. . . . Then he shall come out to the altar that is before the Lord and make atonement for it. . . . He shall sprinkle some of the blood on it with his finger seven times to cleanse it and consecrate it from the uncleanness of the Israelites." Leviticus 16:17-19

The sanctuary itself was to be cleansed from the sins of the people and by that act those sins were removed forever: atonement was completed for the "whole community of Israel". Those sins, however, did not simply vanish into thin air.

"He is to lay both hands on the head of the live goat and confess over it all the wickedness and rebellion of the Israelites - all their sins - and put them on the goat's head. He shall send the goat away into the desert in the care of a man appointed for the task. The goat will carry on itself all their sins to a solitary place and the man shall release it in the desert." Leviticus 16:20-22

At first glance this seems like a beautiful picture of what Jesus has done for us, but on closer study the symbol is flawed. The whole essence of the rest of the sacrificial system is that the Lamb of God is sacrificed, that blood is shed, and "without the shedding of blood there is no forgiveness."[1] How can a goat which does not die be a symbol of Jesus?

In terms of symbol, every man who sinned confessed his wrongs over a live animal which was then killed. By its blood the guilt of sin was transferred to the sanctuary, the dwelling place of God[2] and was stored there[3] until the next Day of Atonement when it was finally removed by the scapegoat who was expelled from the congregation and from God's presence.

We may interpret the symbols thus: every person who sins confesses his wrong to Jesus Christ Who has already died for us. By his death the guilt of our sin is taken from us and placed upon Jesus, Who is in the presence of God. That is how things stand until the cosmic Day of Atonement when the guilt is finally removed and placed upon the scapegoat who then bears it away from God and His people.

Who, then, is the scapegoat? It cannot be Jesus, for He will be forever in the presence of God, to receive the eternal praise and worship of His people. Nor do I believe that any holy creature, whether redeemed man or unfallen angel, is called upon to bear so terrible a burden for eternity. I do not even believe that it will be a fallen man, for each un-redeemed sinner will have enough to do to bear the guilt of his own unforgiven sins.

The most obvious candidate must surely be the originator of sin, the devil himself. Here is the one who is responsible for every sin that has ever been committed, for he has tempted and encouraged every cruel wrong since sin first began. Often enough he has blamed God for the misfortunes of life and has led men to make the same mistake. Now, before the universe, Satan is to be shown in his true colours, the author of all evil, the one responsible for all guilt.

The Hebrew word rendered "reconsecrated" in Daniel 8:14 is perhaps better translated as "justified" or even "vindicated". God and His dealings with His creatures is to be vindicated by the events of the cosmic Day of Atonement.[4]

In Daniel chapter 7 we are presented with the spectacle of a judgement in heaven, a judgement that precedes Christ's investiture as King of kings and Lord of lords. Books or records are opened and the judgement proceeds on the basis of those records.

Drawing all these strands together we find that Daniel 7 describes a pre-Advent judgement. Daniel 8 tells us that the sanctuary will be vindicated at the end of the 2,300 years. The symbolism of the Jewish festivals shows us that before the saints enter the heavenly Canaan there is a solemn time of judgement, the Day of Atonement. The description of that service makes it plain that the guilt of sin is placed on the scapegoat and forever removed during the Day of Atonement.

I believe that in 1844 the cosmic Day of Atonement began in heaven.[5] The heavenly books of record were opened and God began to reveal to the "sons of God" the secrets of His dealings with men. God, Who desires love from all His creatures, submits Himself to the judgement of unfallen intelligences and by them is vindicated against all the false charges of the "father of lies".

When the whole universe can intelligently say "Just and true are Your ways, King of the Ages"[6] then Jesus is crowned Lord of All and comes to claim His inheritance.[7]

On earth the beginning of this judgement was marked by a fresh impetus in the controversy between Christ and Satan. Satan, knowing that the last stages of earth's history had begun, mounted the most subtle and effective attacks on the Bible through the teaching of evolution and the apparent findings of science. Today these have almost reclaimed Christendom for heathendom.

At the same time he raised up counterfeit religions which have also played their part in undermining Christianity. Perhaps most effective of all, he diverted men's attention away from spiritual concerns to social injustices which could only be corrected through politics and revolution.

God's response has been a revival of religion and particularly a revival of interest in the doctrine of the second coming of Christ. The Holy Spirit has led in renewed missionary endeavour to bring the news of Christ's soon coming to every nation of the world in order that men and women might be warned that history is soon to end.

Today, as never before, we are faced with the question "Who is on the Lord's side?" When the judgement ends, will we be found among those who joyfully acknowledge the justice and goodness of God? Do we testify to God's sovereignty now, that we might be judged worthy citizens of His kingdom in the hereafter? John describes those who are faithful in the last days like this:

"Then the dragon was enraged at the woman and went off to make war against the rest of her offspring - those who obey God's commandments and hold to the testimony of Jesus." Revelation 12:17

---

1. Hebrews 9:22

2. It cannot be emphasised too strongly that the sanctuary was indeed the dwelling place of God. Unlike a church or a synagogue, God was actually, physically (if that is the right term to use of God!) present in the Most Holy Place. The glory of the Shekinah revealed God's Presence, as did the fate of Nadab, Abihu and Uzzah who ventured unprepared into that Presence.

3. Some may be disturbed at the thought that the uncleanness of sin could be "stored" in the presence of God. Such people will probably hold that God is too pure to endure sin. It is instructive to remember that sin began in the presence of God and that Satan had visiting rights in heaven after his fall.

4. The book of Job throws an interesting light on the way in which God deals with Satan. In the first chapter of that book we are told of a day when the "sons of God" come together. If these are the "sons of God" who shouted for joy at creation (Job 38:7) then we have a picture of a great meeting or council in heaven when all of God's creatures except fallen man are present.

At that council Satan also appears and God mentions Job as one human who is faithful to God. At once Satan attempts to belittle the claim and declares that Job is only faithful for what he gets out of the relationship and so God allows the fearful test that follows.

The question is: for whose benefit was the test allowed? God, of course, knew already what the outcome would be, for God is omniscient. Satan, the father of lies and a determined rebel, is unlikely to have benefitted in any way by the test. Job was already perfect, so he also did not benefit by this trial of his faith.

That leaves only the "sons of God" as the possible beneficiaries of this test. God wanted to show them that His claims were correct. He wanted to show them that Job served Him for love and not for money. He wanted to vindicate Himself before the unfallen beings of the universe from Satan's charges.

5. 1844 or thereabouts. As no earthly event is predicted it is impossible to demonstrate the exact fulfilment of the date and therefore I cannot believe that the exact day or year is important. The date the Millerites settled upon was October 23, 1844 and as it is based upon sound scholarship and is as good as any other I have no hesitation in accepting it.

6. Revelation 15:3

7. If, as I believe, the pre-Advent judgement began in 1844 then that alone must indicate that we are nearing the Second Coming of Jesus. Although God Himself may live outside of time and a thousand years appear to Him as a single day, yet His creatures do not and it is they who are doing the judging. Soon the last record will be examined and the last verdict given. Soon that final book will be closed and Jesus will be crowned as King. Are you ready to meet Him? Have you placed your guilt on Him, to be dealt with by the cosmic Day of Atonement? If not, then do it now, for when that time comes the door of mercy will be forever shut.

"Let him who does wrong continue to do wrong; let him who is vile continue to be vile; let him who does right continue to do right and let him who is holy continue to be holy." Revelation 22:11

DANIEL

Chapter 10

The final vision of the book of Daniel was given in the third year of the reign of Cyrus. Cyrus is here identified as "king of Persia" rather than as "king of Babylon", making it is impossible to be certain which year should mark the beginning of his reign. Presumably the "third year" is the third year after his conquest of Babylon rather than the third year after he ascended the Persian throne.[1] If so then this vision was given in 536 BC.

According to the chronology adopted here, Darius reigned in Babylon for at least one year, which was probably the year 538/537 BC. This would make 536 BC the first year of Cyrus as king of Babylon and therefore the year in which he issued his decree allowing the Jews to return to Jerusalem. It would seem, however, that he did not come easily to this decision. There may have been a promising start and then the idea seemed to lose favour.

"'At that time I, Daniel, mourned for three weeks. I ate no choice food; no meat or wine touched my lips and I used no lotions at all until the three weeks were over.'" Daniel 10:2, 3

According to Daniel's calculations, based on the prophet Jeremiah, this year marked the end of the seventy years of captivity. Apparently, however, there was no sign in the court circles that Cyrus would fulfil his divine commission and set God's people free. As before, Daniel took the matter to God in prayer and as before he was answered by a vision.

"'On the twenty-fourth day of the first month, as I was standing on the bank of the great river, the Tigris, I looked up and there before me was a man dressed in linen with a belt *of the finest gold round his waist. His body was like chrysolite, his face like lightning, his eyes like flaming torches, his arms and legs like the gleam of burnished bronze and his voice like the sound of a multitude.'" Daniel 10:4-6²*

Although Daniel alone saw this wonderful being, the invisible presence created a supernatural atmosphere of awe which caused Daniel's companions to flee in terror.³ On Daniel himself the effect was more marked.

"'I had no strength left, my face turned deathly pale and I was helpless. Then I heard him speaking and as I listened to him I fell into a deep sleep, my face to the ground.'" Daniel 10:8, 9

Daniel's visitor first strengthened him and then assured him that his prayer had been heard as soon as it was uttered. There had been no need for the three weeks of fasting. The delay in answering Daniel's petition had not been on God's part but on the part of man. Cyrus had resisted the will of God for twenty-one days.⁴ Now, however, the opposition had been overcome and the angel came to Daniel with a message about the future.

"'"Now I have come to explain to you what will happen to your people in the future, for the vision concerns a time yet to come."'" Daniel 10:14

This tells us that the vision that follows was intended to reveal to Daniel the future of his people. Primarily, of course, Daniel's people were the Jews, the descendants of Abraham. When the Jews rejected and crucified the Messiah their period of probation came to an end and their temple and their nation was destroyed.

Paul makes it plain that the true children of Abraham are those who respond to God as Abraham did.

"Understand, then, that those who believe are the children of Abraham. . . . If you belong to Christ then you are Abraham's seed, and heirs according to the promise." Galatians 3:7, 29

As we shall see, the vision of chapter eleven predicts events that occurred well after the destruction of Jerusalem and which are difficult to understand in terms of the history of the Jews, yet which are easily explicable in terms of the history of the Christian church, God's new people.

---

1. If we dated this vision to the third year of Cyrus' reign over Persia we would have to place it before the visions of chapters 8 and 9, in other words, about the year 547 BC.

2. There is an interesting parallel between this vision and that of Revelation chapter 10, which will be discussed later on. For the moment simply notice that the description of Daniel's heavenly visitor is very similar to the description of Jesus in Revelation chapter 1.

3. Normally the visual and auditory centres of our brain are fed signals by the nerves from

our eyes and ears. I have often considered that visions occurred when God fed stimulii directly into the prophet's nerve pathways, bypassing the eyes and ears.

We might take the analogy of a television set which normally receives its electrical signals through an aerial and a UHF decoder. One day, however, the owner disconnects the aerial lead and instead feeds signals in directly from a video recorder or from a video camera.

The fact that Daniel's companions felt a sense of awe amounting to terror might indicate that in some sense the events of the vision actually happened rather than being merely presented to the prophet like a video film. Perhaps this glorious being was really there in front of Daniel and instead of the prophet being miraculously enabled to see what was not there, his companions were miraculously with-held from seeing what was there.

4. Actually, the term "prince of the Persian kingdom" may refer to a spirit being rather than to Cyrus in the same way as Michael is referred to as "one of the chief princes". As this opponent is unlikely to have been one of God's agencies (and was in any case "prince" over a heathen kingdom) we may have a picture of the devil's machinations in resisting God's plans. Nevertheless, the battle raged in the hearts of men, for this heavenly being was "detained there with the king of Persia" (Daniel 10:13)

DANIEL

Chapter 11

" ' "Now then, I tell you the truth. Three more kings will appear in Persia and then a fourth who will be far richer than all the others. When he has gained power by his wealth he will stir up everyone against the kingdom of Greece." ' " Daniel 11:2

This vision was given in the reign of Cyrus. After his death in battle against tribesmen in the north, Cyrus' son Cambysses succeeded to the throne. He died in the course of a successful conquest of Egypt and was followed by the short reign of an imposter known to history as the False Smerdis. The imposter was killed by Darius, the author of the famous inscription on the rock at Behistun. These are the three kings after Cyrus.

Darius attempted an invasion of Greece but was roundly defeated on the plain of Marathon. Xerxes, his successor, determined to complete the work and harnessed the might of his empire to conquer Greece. An army of a million men, drawn from every part of the vast Persian empire, marched into Europe. Herodotus describes how they even drank the streams dry, so great were the numbers in the army.

" ' "Then a mighty king will appear who will rule with great power and do as he pleases. After he has appeared his empire will be broken up and parcelled out towards the four winds of heaven. It will not go to his descendants, nor will it have the power he exercised, because his empire will be uprooted and given to others." ' " Daniel 10:3, 4

Although the Persian empire continued for another 120 years after Xerxes, it is impossible to discover in its history an individual who could fulfill the details of this prediction. On the other hand these verses are a very good description of the career of Alexander the Great. It would seem that the angel skipped over the later kings of Persia, missing out over a century of human history, to go directly to the first great king of the Greek empire.

This brings us to an important principle in the interpretation of Daniel chapter 11. Whenever a new power is introduced which will thereafter rule over God's people, the line of thought immediately leaves the previous power and concerns itself exclusively with the new one. This peculiarity has been often overlooked by expositors, with curious results in their interpretations of the chapter.

Alexander the Great conquered the Persian empire in a swift series of battles between 333 and 331 BC, but at the height of his success he died in Babylon leaving only an infant son who quickly disappeared - probably murdered. Almost immediately Alexander's kingdom was divided among his generals, the four divisions depicted by the four heads of the leopard of chapter 7.

""The king of the south will become strong, but one of his commanders will become even stronger than he and will rule his own kingdom with great power."'" Daniel 11:5

The "king of the south" can only refer to Ptolemy I Soter[1], the general who seized the rich land of Egypt. Not only was this to the south of the Holy Land, the usual Biblical reference point, but it was also the southernmost of the Greek kingdoms. The "king of the north" who is mentioned in the next verse is the king of Syria, the Seleucid kingom.

Ptolemy I gave refuge to Seleucus I Nicator, the satrap of Babylon, who fled to Egypt to escape awkward questions concerning his administration of Babylonia. After serving Ptolemy for four years he returned to Babylon and captured the city with a small army. From there he defied all attempts to destroy him and eventually was able to start a career of conquest towards the east that was only halted when he met Chandragupta, the founder of the Maurya dynasty in India.

Thwarted in the east Seleucus turned to the west and defeated Antigonus and Lysimachus, adding Syria, Asia Minor and Greece to his empire. No wonder the angel declared that "one of his commanders will become even stronger than he." Seleucus was assassinated in 281 BC and his kingdom passed to his son Antiochus I.

""After some years they will become allies. The daughter of the king of the south will go to the king of the north to make an alliance but she will not retain her power and he and his power will not last. In those days she will be handed over, together with her royal escort and her child and the one who supported her."'" Daniel 11:6

The hostilities between the Ptolemies and the Seleucids over Syria continued. Ptolemy II Philadelphus[2] determined to settle the quarrel and made peace with Antiochus II Theos. To seal the treaty Antiochus was required to divorce his wife Laodice and marry Ptolemy's daughter Berenice, thus disinheriting Laodice's sons.

This Antiochus duly did, but in such an arranged, dynastic marriage, there was no question of love and very shortly Laodice and her sons were back in court. Laodice, however, was not prepared to overlook the insult she had received and soon afterwards was successful in poisoning Antiochus and murdering Berenice and her entourage. Laodice' son, Seleucus II Callinichus, became the next king of Syria.

"'One from her family line will arise to take her place. He will attack the forces of the king of the north and enter his fortress: he will fight against them and be victorious. He will also seize their gods, their metal images and their valuable articles of silver and gold and carry them off to Egypt. For some years he will leave the king of the north alone. Then the king of the north will invade the realm of the king of the south but will retreat to his own country."' Daniel 11:7-9

Berenice' brother, Ptolemy III Euergetes, invaded Syria to avenge his sister's death and succeeded in capturing the Syrian capital Seleucia. He killed Laodice and raided into Mesopotamia where he was able to regain for Egypt a number of images carried away by the Persian Cambyses. This won him immense popularity in Egypt and when he founded the famous temple at Edfu a special order of priests were set up to worship him and his wife.

Seleucus II Callinichus, with the help of allies from the Black Sea region, was able to recover Mesopotamia and most of northern Syria and win a peace treaty with Egypt. This may be the "invasion" referred to in verse 9. However other enemies carried on the war and Seuelucus II died in exile of a fall from his horse and was succeeded by his son Seleucus III Soter. After an inglorious reign of just three years he was murdered and was followed by his brother, Antiochus III the Great.

"'His sons will prepare for war and assemble a great army which will sweep on like an irresistible flood and carry the battle as far as his fortress. Then the king of the south will march out in rage and fight against the king of the north, who will raise a large army but it will be defeated. When the army is carried off, the king of the south will be filled with pride and will slaughter many thousands yet he will not remain triumphant."' Daniel 11:10-12

Antiochus the Great attacked Egypt but was obliged to break off hostilities to deal with a domestic revolt. It was obvious that he intended to continue the war as soon as opportunity afforded. Both sides prepared their armies and when Antiochus invaded Egyptian territory, after some initial successes he was decisively defeated at the battle of Raphia with the loss of 14,000 killed.

Ptolemy IV Philopator, a pleasure loving puppet in the hands of his drinking companions, lacked the energy to profit by his victory. He made peace easily, thus leaving Antiochus to rebuild his strength for another attack. Ptolemy IV died leaving a 5 year old son. The drinking companions quickly murdered the child's mother and appointed themselves as his guardians. During this period of weakness and confusion Antiochus saw his opportunity.

" " For the king of the north will muster another army, larger than the first; and after several years he will advance with a huge army fully equipped." " Daniel 11:13

Instead of invading Egypt, however, Antiochus contented himself with conquering Ptolemaic lands in Asia Minor. The war was concluded after the Romans intervened, with Antiochus in by far the stronger position. Ptolemy V is noted in history for two things: he sealed the peace treaty by marrying the daughter of Antiochus, a girl by the name of Cleopatra, thus introducing the name into the Egyptian line; and some priests in a small provincial town by the name of Rosetta set up a stele in three languages to commemorate a royal gift to their foundation.

" " In those times many will rise against the king of the south. The violent men among your own people will rebel in fulfillment of the vision but without success." " Daniel 11:14

While Ptolemy V Epiphanes was still a minor his kingdom was torn apart by revolts and civil war. His father had left the young child to the guardianship of the Romans but even they were not enough to prevent the disasters that befell the Egyptian cause.

M. Emilius Lepidus, a member of the Roman senate, was appointed to educate the king, a task which he delegated to Aristomenes, a trusted courtier of the Alexandrian court. Between them they appointed Scopas, a Greek mercenary, to lead the army, but despite his energy and ability he suffered a humiliating defeat near Banias, fled to Sidon and was forced to surrender to the beseiging forces of Antiochus the Great.

Egypt never again controlled Palestine. Instead the land of Israel came under the control of the Seleucids, and immediately found life much harder. Taxes, which had been low under the lax rule of the Ptolemies, were greatly increased. The Jewish religion was scorned and indeed Josephus informs us that under the rule of Seleucus IV an attempt was made to rob the temple treasury. The Greek agent, the general Heliodorus, was frightened off by a vision of angels who chastised him.

Matters came to a head under Antiochus IV Epiphanes who, in pursuit of a misguided policy of cultural assimilation, forbade the practice of the Jewish religion. The temple services were stopped, the temple itself desecrated by the sacrifice of a pig, and anyone who observed the Sabbath, circumcised his children or kept the Torah was put to death.

Many were martyred, willingly facing the most horrendous tortures rather than deny their faith. Others were made of sterner stuff. When Antiochus' agents came to Modein, about 18 miles north west of Jerusalem, they were killed by Matthias and his five sons who then started a guerilla war against the Greeks.

For a while the fortunes of war favoured neither side, but then Matthias died and his son Judas succeeded him as leader of the struggle. He was so successful that he received the nick-name "Maccabaeus" or "hammer", a name which was given to the dynasty he founded.[3]

Jerusalem was cleansed by the victorious Jews who, however, found themselves faced with a problem. The fire on the altar was polluted and extinguished, but who was worthy to re-kindle the fire of God? The problem was solved when, behind a bricked up wall, a lamp was found still burning after three years. Jews still celebrate Hanukkah, the Festival of Light, to commemorate this miraculous event.

"'"Then the king of the north will come and build up siege ramps and will capture a fortified city. The forces of the south will be powerless to resist; even their best troops will not have the strength to stand."'" Daniel 11:15

Antiochus' attacks on the Jews may have stemmed from an event just a little earlier in his reign. He attacked Egypt and defeated the Egyptian army so soundly that he actually captured the whole country apart from Alexandria. He was in Eleusis, one of the suburbs of Alexandria, when Gaius Popillius Laenas, the Roman ambassador, found him and demanded that he withdraw from Egypt which was under Roman protection.

Antiochus used the common eastern ploy of promising to consider the matter and give an answer in due course. The Roman, however, drew a circle around the king with his staff and demanded an answer before Antiochus left the circle. Knowing the Roman power (he had been a hostage in Rome for many years) Antiochus was forced to agree to their demands, but his humiliation made him eager to humiliate someone else.

The years following the death of Antiochus IV saw increasing weakness in the Seleucid empire as kings fought pretenders for the throne only to be murdered by rival brothers. Through it all, with considerable skill, the Maccabees, or Hasmonaeans as they came to be called, continued to build up their strength until at last it seemed that Judea had gained complete freedom under John Hyrcanus, perhaps the greatest of the Hasmonaeans.

Early in his reign the Seleucid throne was taken by Antiochus VII, the last strong Syrian king. He determined to recapture Palestine and swept south to beseige Jerusalem. After resisting for more than a year Hyrcanus was forced to surrender, but received surprisingly lenient terms and continued to rule.

When Antiochus VII was assassinated not long afterwards Hyrcanus was able to expand his kingdom by conquering Samaria and Idumea.[4] The Hasmonaean kingdom became ever more powerful, though with an underlying thread of violence at the top. One claimant to the throne starved his mother to death. Another murdered his imprisoned brother to ensure his own succession.

"'"The invader will do as he pleases; no-one will be able to stand against him. He will establish himself in the Beautiful Land and will have the power to destroy it."'" Daniel 11:16

Eventually two brothers, in outright war with each other, invited the Roman general Pompey to adjudicate their claims. Pompey, on his way back from defeating the kings of Pontus and Armenia, was only too glad of this excuse to intervene in yet another country. He entered Palestine, beseiged Jerusalem and captured it and even dared to enter the Holy of Holies, finding to his bewilderment that it was totally empty and bare. From this point on the prophecy concerns itself with the history of Rome in the Middle East.

From this verse onwards there is no mention of the familiar kings of north and south until near the end of the chapter. Instead the prophecy's attention is focussed on "he". Applying the principle mentioned earlier, that once a new power is introduced the prophecy concerns itself exclusively with this new power, we must assume that the "he" is the Roman empire in the guise of its various rulers. The "he" who enters and controls the "Beautiful Land" is Pompey.

"'"He will determine to come with the might of his entire kingdom and will make an alliance with the king of the south. And he will give him a daughter in marriage in order to overthrow the kingdom but she will not succeed or help him."'" Daniel 11:17

Pompey fell victim to the machinations of his rivals in the power politics of Rome. He fled for refuge to various kings whom he had befriended in the east, but eventually was betrayed and killed on the shore of Egypt near Alexandria. A monument called Pompey's Pillar is supposed to mark the spot where the great general was beheaded.

Julius Caesar came to power in Rome and soon turned towards the east to bolster the reputation gained in Gaul. In Egypt, posing as friend and protector of the young Ptolemy, Julius Caesar made a treaty with the young ruler - a treaty that was quickly forgotten, however, when the young man's sister was smuggled naked into Caesar's presence in a rolled up carpet.

The Hebrew term translated "daughter" is really a phrase: "the daughter of women". Just as "son of man" indicates a typical man or the epitome of manhood, so "daughter of women" indicates the epitome of womanhood, a fitting description of Cleopatra who, through force of personality rather than physical beauty, succeeded in enslaving Julius Caesar.

"'"Then he will turn his attention to the coastlands and will take many of them, but a commander will put an end to his insolence and will turn his insolence back upon him. After this he will turn back towards the fortresses of his own country but will stumble and fall, to be seen no more."'" Daniel 11:18, 19

War in Syria and Asia Minor drew Julius Caesar away from Egypt. He fought against Pharnaces, king of the country around the Bosphorus and defeated him in a single battle, so that Caesar was moved to utter his famous epigram: "Veni, vidi, vici - I came, I saw, I conquered." He returned to Rome and there, in fancied safety and security he was assassinated. One of the reasons for this assassination was that the Romans feared that Caesar wanted to become king and the the Romans had lively memories of the insolent and tyrannical behaviour of their last king.

"'"His successor will send out a tax collector to maintain the royal splendour. In a few years, however, he will be destroyed, yet not in anger or in battle."'" Daniel 11:20

Julius Caesar's death was followed by a short-lived triumvirate of Octavius, Mark Antony and Lepidus who united to avenge their patron's death but then fought amongst themselves until only Octavius was left. The Roman Senate conferred the title "Augustus" on him, and it is by this name that he is mentioned in Luke.

"In those days Caesar Augustus issued a decree that a census should be taken of the entire Roman world." Luke 2:1

A census and a taxing were one and the same thing. Most people, from often repitition during Christmas, know that Augustus was famous for his taxations, the other events of his long and illustrious reign are forgotten. He died peacefully in his bed at the age of seventy-six.

"'"He will be succeeded by a contemptible person who has not been given the honour of royalty. He will invade[5] the kingdom when its people feel secure and he will seize it through intrigue."'" Daniel 11:21

Augustus was followed by Tiberius, thanks to the intrigues of his mother, Augustus' wife. The Emperor Nero has the popular name for cruelty and dissipation and deservedly so, but whereas Nero's vices were public Tiberius was as bad, but in private. He retreated to the island of Capri and there indulged in cruel murders and unspeakable sexual perversions until his death.

" ' "Then an overwhelming army will be swept away before him: both it and a prince of the covenant will be destroyed." ' " Daniel 11:22

The "prince of the covenant" is, in my opinion, undoubtedly the same as the "anointed one (or Messiah), the prince" of chapter nine. Again Luke gives us the neccessary chronological information.

"In the fifteenth year of the reign of Tiberius Caesar - when Pontius Pilate was governor of Judea . . . . - the word of God came to John son of Zechariah in the desert." Luke 3:1, 2

In other words, during the reign of Tiberius Jesus began His public ministry and three and a half years later was crucified.

Up to this point interpreters of Daniel chapter eleven have been divided into two main groups. One group, the traditionalists, follow fairly closely to the interpretation given above. The second group apply all this, in one way or another, to the career of the various Syrian and Egyptian kings. From now on, however, interpretations begin to vary widely, often becoming fanciful in the extreme.

The key to the matter lies in recognising that a new power has been introduced - the Christian church. Faithful to the principle mentioned previously, the prophecy passes over the intervening rulers of the Roman empire and goes directly to the time when the Christian church begins to have a measure of political power - the conversion of Constantine.

" ' "After coming to an agreement with him, he will act deceitfully and with only a few people he will rise to power. When the richest provinces feel secure he will invade them and will achieve what neither his fathers nor his forefathers did. He will distribute plunder, loot and wealth among his followers. He will plot the overthrow of fortresses - but only for a time." ' " Daniel 11:23, 24

When the Roman empire came to an agreement with the persecuted Christian church the Christians rejoiced in their freedom to worship God and to preach to the heathen. It wasn't long, however, before the church began to seek after power and in Constantine's lifetime there was persecution of Christian by Christian, with the Donatists of north Africa being deprived of their liberty and even their lives.

As the Roman empire disintegrated before the attacks of the barbarians so the church gained in political power. What was worse was that it began to regard this power as its right until the bishop of Rome claimed supremacy over all the kings of the earth and sought to enforce that supremacy with the spiritual weapon of excommunication and when that failed with the wordly weapons of intrigue and armed might.

The various church taxes, offerings and dues resulted in the wealth of the nations pouring into Rome where it was used to support the extravagent lifestyle of popes, cardinals and bishops. Country after country found it neccessary to prohibit by law the transfer of gold and silver to Rome and the giving of gifts to churches and monasteries.

""' With a large army he will stir up his strength and courage against the king of the south. The king of the south will wage war with a large and very powerful army but he will not be able to stand because of the plots devised against him. Those who eat from the king's provisions will try to destroy him; his army will be swept away and many will fall in battle."'" Daniel 11:25, 26

Once the church had established itself securely in Europe it was free to turn its attention to the Holy Land which had been conquered by the Muslims. At this time the seat of Muslim power was in Egypt. Although the first Crusades attacked the Muslims in Palestine, subsequent crusades headed directly for Egypt.

Though the prophecy does not make it clear who was the victim of the plots - the king of the south or the invading "he" - history is clear that the crusaders were defeated. Twice the crusaders invaded Egypt, twice they besieged Damietta and twice they were defeated by divided leadership and ill-advised counsels.

"'"The two kings, with their hearts bent on evil, will sit at the same table and lie to each other, but to no avail, because an end will still come at the appointed time."'" Daniel 11:27

The closing years of the Crusader period produced no such paladins of chivalry and nobility as Salah-ud-Din and Richard the Lion Heart. Instead we find a constant thread of treachery running through the dealings of Christian and Muslim, culminating in the perfidious treaties made by Sultan Baybars (no doubt he regarded them as good military strategy) that led to the extermination of the Latin Kingdom.

"'"The king of the north will return to his own country with great wealth but his heart will be set against the holy covenant. He will take action against it and then return to his own country."'" Daniel 11:28

Historians may be divided about the impact of the Crusades on the East but there is no doubt of the impact of the East on the Crusaders. Returned Crusaders brought with them a flood of new ideas, a host of new trading connections and a desire for higher standards of living. The Crusades played an important part in breaking up the feudal system and gave increased prosperity to the towns and the "middle" class - midway between villein and lord.

Although Crusades in the Holy Land were no longer a military possibility, the concept of a crusade - an armed expedition in defense of the church - remained alive. The Roman Catholic church used it to mount wars of extermination against various groups of which it disapproved. Simon de Montfort (father of the man so famous in English politics) led the first of these, the crusade against the Albigenses of Languedoc in southern France, 1209-1229. Smaller crusades in later years attacked the Waldenses of northern Italy and the Hussites of Bavaria.[6]

"'"At the appointed time he will invade the south again, but this time the outcome will be different from what it was before. Ships of the western coastlands will oppose him and he will lose heart. Then he will turn back and vent his fury against the holy covenant. He will return and show favour to those who forsake the holy covenant."'" Daniel 11:29, 30

There is no indication as to the identity of this "appointed time" and the phrase may mean no more than that the attack will happen at the time foreseen by God.[7] In 1270 the last crusade took place when Louis IX of France attacked, as he thought, the power of Egypt by an invasion of Tunis. This may be the invasion different from the previous ones.

The struggle between Christian and Muslim became a succession of actions at sea. Two in particular stand out: the sea-borne invasion of Malta by the Turkish admiral Barbarossa, which was defeated by the heroism of the Knights of St John; and the historic Battle of Lepanto when the Turkish navy was decisively defeated by the galleys of Christendom.

From this time on the Roman Catholic church became increasingly concerned with earthly power. Theological views were adopted and taught that tended to magnify the role of the church and its officers - the priests and prelates. Such doctrines as the doctrine of papal supremacy, the doctrine of transubstantiation, the doctrine of auricular confession and the doctrines of purgatory and indulgences gave great power to the priest.

During this time anyone who could serve the ambitions of the papacy was flattered and encouraged, no matter how evil their lives might be. Kings and emperors were used and encouraged or stricken with anathemas, not for the piety or sinfulness of their lives but because of their usefulness or otherwise to the political aims of the church.

"'"His armed forces will rise up to desecrate the temple fortress and will abolish the daily sacrifice. Then they will set up the abomination that causes desolation."'" Daniel 11:31

Naturally these false doctrines could not be found in the Bible and so recourse was had to heathen philosophies and "science" to provide a basis for them.[8] For example, the doctrine of transubstantiation is founded upon Plato's theory about the divine world of "ideas" and the imperfect world of "accidents".

As heathen ideas crept in the Church became more and more corrupt both in doctrine and in practice and the true worship of God ceased. Arms and force were used against those who sought to keep to the purity of Biblical Christianity. The blood of massacres and the flames of the Inquisition instituted a reign of terror in the place of Christ's reign of peace.

"'"With flattery he will corrupt those who have violated the covenant, but the people who know their God will firmly resist him. Those who are wise will instruct many, though for a time they will fall by the sword or be burned or captured or plundered."'" Daniel 11:32

On the other hand, those who conformed and supported the papacy in its pretensions could gain rich rewards - bishoprics, arch-bishoprics and cardinalates or simply the overflowing coffers of Tetzel the indulgence pedlar. Greed was a motive well understood by those who elected the Borgias to power.

This is not the biased invective of a Protestant. Boccacio, the staunch Catholic writer of risque tales, tells of a Jew who went to Rome and observed the greed and corruption rampant in the heart of Christendom and was converted as a result! His reasoning was simple: despite the assiduity with which everyone from the pope downwards endeavoured to destroy Christianity, the church continued to grow and prosper. Obviously therefore God was favouring the Christians!

Not all who chronicled the evils of their time were content to divert their minds with lustful fantasies. God raised up men who called for reform, men such as Jan Huss, Savonarola, John Wyclif, the Waldenses, and doubtless many others whose names are known only to God. Finally came Martin Luther, calling the church to reformation and only when it refused turning to the establishment of a pure church.

The time that followed was a time of renewed persecution. In some cases, such as the St Bartholemew's Day Massacre and the Hugenots, the papacy was successful in stamping out the reform movements. In others, such as the Dutch and the English reformers, the fires of persecution only served to kindle yet brighter flames of zeal and consecration.

"'"When they fall, they will receive a little help and many who are not sincere will join them. Some of the wise will stumble so that they may be refined, purified and made spotless until the time of the end, for it will still come at the appointed time."'" Daniel 11:34, 35

Time and again God intervened to preserve the Protestant reformation. When the Holy Roman emperor Charles V gathered his armies to march against

Luther the Turks attacked Vienna and he was forced to divert his efforts in that direction. When the Spanish sent their Armada against England the winds destroyed the fleet that had been but lightly touched by Drake's utmost efforts.

As the Protestant cause prospered so many came to espouse it simply to further their own ambitions. Just as Henry of Navarre turned Catholic because Paris was worth a mass, others went in the opposite direction just as lightly and gradually the purity and zeal of the reformation became dull formalism, as displeasing to God as that which it had replaced.

Yet God continued to raise up men and women who kept the Protestant ideals alive - the Covenanteers in Scotland, John Bunyan in Bedford gaol, the Wesleys, George Fox and George Whitefield - until it burst across the globe in the great explosion of missionary activity that saw Christianity taken to the furthest reaches of the earth.

"'"The king will do as he pleases. He will exalt and magnify himself above every god and will say unheard-of things against the God of gods. He will be successful until the time of wrath is completed, for what has been determined must take place. He will show no regard for the gods of his fathers or for the one desired by women, nor will he regard any god, but will exalt himself above them all. Instead of them he will honour a god of fortresses; a god unknown to his fathers he will honour with gold and silver, with precious stones and costly gifts. He will attack the mightiest fortresses with the help of a foreign god and will greatly honour those who acknowledge him. He will make them rulers over many people and will distribute the land at a price."'" Daniel 11:36-39

At this point in the prophecy we are approaching our own day and it is well for us to realise that events which seem to us to hold great significance may, in God's estimation, be only passing disturbances in some grand historical process of which we are unaware. A prime example of this is Uriah Smith, the 19th century expositor, who interpreted the whole of this last part of Daniel 11 in terms of the career of Napoleon, with emphasis on his invasion of Egypt. Today we are able to assess the French invasion of Egypt as a minor adventure which produced no lasting results.

The traditional interpretation has been to regard verses 36 to 39 as a recapping of the iniquities of the papacy. In my opinion this is mistaken. We have passed the point at which the papacy has been weakened by the Reformation. The blatant corruption of medieval times has passed away and while there may well still be individuals who are evil (and one thinks of the recent revelations about the Vatican's financial dealings) the Protestant world has too many such individuals of its own for it to point the finger of opprobrium at the Catholics.

Another alternative is to look at the way in which Protestant churches have become cold and formal. This is even less satisfactory because the terms of the prophecy indicates political power with phrases such as "the king", "attack the mightiest fortresses" and "make them rulers". On the whole, Protestant churches hold to the principle of the separation between church and state and do not seek political power.

The clue, it seems to me, lies in the two phrases "nor will he regard any god" and "a god unknown to his fathers will he honour". I believe that athiestic communism fulfills the specifications of this prophecy. It blasphemes against the God of heaven, it rejects all gods yet at the same time elevates the theories of Marx and Lenin to the status of religions. Its wealth is spent on armaments, it seeks conquest by force and those who join the communist party do indeed receive honours. One of the major aims of communism party is the re-distribution of land.[9]

"'"At the time of the end the king of the south will engage him in battle, and the king of the north will storm out against him with chariots and cavalry and a great fleet of ships. He will invade many countries and sweep through them like a flood. He will also invade the Beautiful Land. Many countries will fall, but Edom, Moab and the leaders of Ammon will be delivered from his hand. He will extend his power over many countries; Egypt will not escape. He will gain control of the treasures of gold and silver and all the riches of Egypt, with the Libyans and Nubians in submission."'" Daniel 11:40-43

Our interpretation of this passage depends upon our identification of the "him". That is, do the kings of north and south attack a third party or is the power of the preceeding verses the king of the north? My opinion is that as the communist powers are almost all to the north of Palestine it is quite safe to identify them collectively (or possibly Russia individually as the leading communist nation) as the "king of the north."

The "king of the south" then may represent either Egypt or the Arab world generally. We have here a picture of conflict between Communism and Islam, either directly or involving a third state, and there is no more suitable candidate for this than the modern State of Israel and its great ally, the Christian United States of America.

Already we see Russia in conflict with renaiscent fundamentalist Islam - the war in Afghanistan and the unrest in the Muslim republic of Azerbaijan may merely be the prelude before the storm. One can think of other reasons beside religion why these two powers may collide, and the oil wealth of the Arab states is the most obvious.

If this interpretation is correct, we can anticipate war breaking out yet again in the Middle East, but this time Russia sends its fleets down through the Dardanelles and invades Palestine. Perhaps because of a treaty, or more likely because the land is not worth troubling about, the invasion spares the modern country of Jordan, but sweeps down through Israel - as a propaganda coup to prove that the Russians are the friends of the Arab cause, and into Egypt. There it is welcomed by the left-wing states of Libya and Nubia.

"'"*But reports from the east and the north will alarm him and he will set out in a great rage to destroy and annihilate many. He will pitch his royal tents between the seas at the beautiful holy mountain. Yet he will come to his end and no-one will help him.*"'"
Daniel 11:44, 45

However the invasion ends unexpectedly. Either there is trouble inside Russia itself or the Chinese to the east and the Americans, via the North Pole route for their missiles, intervene. The Russian army adopts its age-old practice of killing everything that moves, this time perhaps aided by the horrors of nuclear war, but to no avail. World War III breaks out as the Russians are decisively defeated.

Let me emphasise again that this is how I interpret the prophecy in the light of the present political situation.[10] I believe that we are very near the end of time and that therefore the present is the probable setting for the last verses of Daniel 11. I may be wrong; there may yet be many decades of history before Christ returns. Let the reader keep his eyes open for the fulfilment of this prophecy. Watch for the signs of the times that these events, however they work out, do not pass by unnoticed.

All I would add is the sobering thought that the hill of Megiddo - Armageddon in Hebrew - is only a couple of minutes from Jerusalem as the MIG flies.

---

1. To attempt to make these confusing kings clearer, here is a table of the kings of Egypt and Syria.

Syria		Egypt	
Seleucus I Nicator	312-281	Ptolemy I Soter	323-285
Antiochus I Soter	281-261	Ptolemy II Philadelphus	285-246
Antiochus II Theos	261-246	Ptolemy III Euergetes	246-221
Seleucus II Callinicus	246-225	Ptolemy IV Philopator	221-205
Seleucus III Soter	225-223	Ptolemy V Epiphanes	205-180
Antiochus III Magnus	223-187	Ptolemy VI Philometor	180-145
Seleucus IV	187-175	Ptolemy VII Neos Philopator	145-144
Antiochus IV Ephiphanes	175-164	Ptolemy VIII Euergetes	144-116
Antiochus V	164-162	Ptolemy IX Soter	116- 80
Demetrius I	162-150	Ptolemy X Alexander	107- 88
Alexander Balas	150-145	Ptolemy XI Alexander	81- 80
Demetrius II	145-139	Ptolemy XII Auletes	80- 51
Antiochus VII Sidetes	139-129	Ptolemy XIII Theos Philopator	51- 47
Antiochus XIII	69- 64	Cleopatra	

2. This Ptolemy was not only, as his name implies, a lover of his fellow men, but also a lover of knowledge. He was exceedinly proud of his library and lost no opportunity to add to it. Hearing that the Jews possessed a holy book of great antiquity and wisdm, he invited a delegation to come and translate it into Greek.

According to tradition, seventy men were sent to carry out this commission. Arriving in Alexandria they were feasted and then placed in individual rooms and set to work. After seventy days each man had completed his translation and when the seventy manuscripts were compared, each was word for word identical to all the others.

Whether you believe that tale or not, it is a fact that Ptolemy II was responsible for the Greek translation of the Old Testament which, because of this legend, became known as the Septuagent, the Translation of the Seventy. In fact, it is often referred to by the Roman numerals LXX!

3. The Jews naturally regarded his success against the might of the Seleucid empire as evidence of God's miraculous power. At first the Maccabean rebels did not fight on the Sabbath, but they were massacred by the Greeks who quickly learned that it was easier to fight on a Saturday against enemies who did not resist! After several such disasters, without any deliverance from heaven, the Maccabees granted themselves a dispensation and fought as bravely on the Sabbath as on any other day.

This fact alone may make us wonder whether the Maccabean movement was divinely inspired or whether it was not, as Daniel tells us, "the violent men among your own people." Judas was eventually killed in battle and the Syrians regained temporary control over Jerusalem.

Some of the Jews themselves had similar doubts and eventually many of these left Jerusalem and set up communes of the righteous in the desert. They became the Essenes, the third sect of Judaism and seem to have been responsible for the Qumran settlement and the Dead Sea Scrolls. Their beliefs and practices may be the background against which we should set the coming of John the Baptist.

4. When the Jews were taken into Babylon the Edomites left their rugged desert and settled in the south of Judea where their territory became known as Idumea. When Hyrcanus conquered this area he forced the Edomites to accept the Jewish religion, thus effectively wiping them out as an identifiable culture.

Though he may have congratulated himself on the success of his plan, in fact this action gave a certain Idumean, Antipater by name, the opportunity to rise in the Jewish nation and eventually his son became king and killed the last surviving Hasmonaeans. The son's name was Herod. Religious intolerance and forced conversion do not pay!

5. It is in these and the succeeding verses that we come against the bug-bear of Bible interpreters - the translators. I do not wish to cast any doubts upon the honesty, sincerity or competence of Bible translators - far from it! - but nonetheless they are only human. Faced with a choice of possible renderings for a Hebrew word the translator will naturally opt for that meaning which most closely expresses the Hebrew as he understands it. This is natural and understandable but unfortunately it has the effect of biasing the translation towards a certain interpretation.

The majority of Biblical scholars adopt the view that Daniel is a book written about 164 BC by an unknown author who penned a fictitious account of happenings in far-off Babylon in order to encourage his fellow Jews in their rebellion against Antiochus IV. This means that they interpret the various beasts and predictions of Daniel in terms of events in the Maccabean era.

"Invaded" is a perfectly proper translation of the Hebrew word in this verse, but other, less dramatic renderings are equally proper. There are other instances of this unconscious bias in the verses to follow.

The King James Version of the Bible was translated in 1611 when there was no "orthdox" interpretation of Daniel's prophecies to bias the translation, by men who believed (as I do) that the author was a Jew living in the sixth century BC. Although we must recognise the limitations of the

KJV, particularly in areas where our knowledge has increased thanks to archaeology, no serious student of the Bible can afford to ignore the KJV unless he is able to fluently read Hebrew and Greek for him or her self.

6. Not all these groups were representative of the "Holy Covenant". Although Protestants are proud to number the Waldenses and John Huss as progenitors of the Reformation, most scholars agree that the Albigenses were indeed non-Christian heretics. One must add a caveat to that, however.

According to the records of the Inquisition (which began with St Dominic's endeavours to convert the Albigenses) these Cathars, as they were known, believed in a dualism of good and evil. They were divided into the laity, who could marry and take part worldly affairs and the perfectii or catharii who abstained from marriage and lived ascetic lives. They regarded the world of matter as evil and many catharii committed ritual suicide in order to enter the pure world of the spirit.

This, as I say, is the record of their enemies and sounds pretty damning. However it should not be forgotten that the same enemies, in the service of the king of France, denounced the Knights Templars as heretics anc accused them of various blasphemous practices. Most scholars are now agreed that these charges are at best wild exaggerations and probably complete fabrications. People will admit anything under torture.

It is possible therefore that the Albigenses were not nearly as bad as they are painted or at least that only an unrepresentative few held to these heretical ideas. Not even the Inquisitors could deny that the average Cathar held to a higher moral standard than the Catholics of his time and lived a life worthy of the name of Christian, even if his beliefs were unorthdox.

7. Verse 29 is rather difficult to interpret. The KJV places it as the end of the previous paragraph rather than as the start of a new one, thus the "appointed time" is a parenthetical reference to some future time when the south will again be invaded rather than a statement of events in the direct line of the prophecy.

It is difficult to see why the translators of the NIV have inserted the word "outcome" when the outcome is so manifestly identical to the previous invasion - the invader is defeated and returns to attack the "holy covenant"! The Hebrew simply says, to translate literally, "it shall not be as the former, so the latter".

Finally, the phrase "western coastlands" is an interpretation rather than a translation. The Hebrew actually says "Kittim", which is the name given in the Old Testament to Cyprus. In later times it came to be applied to the islands of the eastern Mediterranean and the Aegean in general and later still it was used as a code word for the Romans.

8. Both Matthew and Mark record that Jesus used the phrase "abomination of desolation" to refer to the Roman armies that surrounded Jerusalem in 70 AD. Bible students agree that in these passages Jesus was speaking both of the events in 70 AD and of the events associated with His second coming. We need not limit our interpretation to the Roman armies that destroyed Jerusalem.

The Hebrew word translated as "abomination" in the verse is used in 1 Kings 11:5-7 and 2 Kings 23:13 to describe the heathen gods of the nations around Israel. (The KJV translates literally "the abomination of the Moabites", etc. whereas the NIV is pleased to add the word "god" - "the vile god of the Moabites" to make the meaning plain.) Elsewhere the word is used exclusively to refer to heathen worship.

It would seem then that the "abomination of desolation" is a heathen worship that results in the desolation of God's people.

9. A good, but to my mind less convincing, case can be made for identifying this power as modern materialistic capitalism. I prefer the communist identification but I refuse to be dogmatic. I have no desire to be a second Uriah Smith in this respect.

10. Since writing these words the situation with regard to Russia as a world power has changed dramatically. The Berlin wall has been demolished, the Warsaw Pact has ceased to be a threat and the USSR itself bids fair to disintegrate into its component republics. In fact, at this precise moment the Iraqis under Saddam Hussein make a more threatening "king of the north" than do the Russians. (To the Jews the king of Babylon was truly the "king of the north" because the Babylonians always invaded from the north.)

These changes merely underline my point, that the student of this part of the prophecy must be awake to events in the world around him, constantly ready to revise and re-interpret his speculations. This is not to live in a fever of millenial expectations but rather to be alert to see the hand of God in history. The Jews of 612 BC merely saw a new twist in the tale of war and bloodshed when Ninevah fell. It was the prophets who discerned that God was preparing to chastise His people for their sins.

It is my personal belief that Saddam Husein will soon join the ranks of ex-dictators and that the situation in the Middle East will return to normal until the next crisis. I may well be wrong, but one thing is certain. I shall be watching events with considerable interest, eagerly waiting for the day when "Michael shall stand up."

DANIEL

Chapter 12

"'"At that time Michael, the great prince who protects your people, will arise. There will be a time of distress such as has not happened from the beginning of nations until then. But at that time your people - everyone whose name is found written in the book - will be delivered. Multitudes who sleep in the dust of the earth will awake: some to everlasting life, others to shame and everlasting contempt."'" Daniel 12:1, 2

When events on earth seem certain to result in the total annihilation of the human race, God intervenes. Michael, the heavenly prince[1], arises to put an end to human strife. The time of distress is caused by the aftermath of war and we may be sure that the devil, knowing that this is his last effort, does his best to persecute and destroy God's people during this time of chaos.

It may be that some who profess to be followers of God will fall before the devil's malice - other Old Testament prophecies[2] speak of the heathen appearing to be victorious - but those who truly belong to God will be safe. Those whose names are written in the Lamb's Book of Life will be delivered.

Then Jesus comes again and the dead come to life: those who have died believing in God receive the gift of never-ending life while those who rejected God awake only to shame and destruction.

"'"Those who impart wisdom will shine like the brightness of the heavens and those who lead many to righteousness like the stars for ever and ever."'" Daniel 12:3

Here is an incentive that should lead us to proclaim the Lordship of Jesus Christ. The honours of the heavenly kingdom are awarded to those who have most effectively and fearlessly led others to receive Jesus as their Saviour.

" ' "But you, Daniel, close up and seal the words of the scroll until the time of the end. Many will go here and there to increase knowledge." ' " Daniel 12:4

The book of Daniel has not always been understood as we are able to understand it. Since it was written Bible students have tried to interpret its symbols with varying degrees of success. Generally when some event has become history it has been correctly identified but attempts to predict the future have almost invariably been wrong - hence my own refusal to be dogmatic!

A big stumbling block has, of course, been the time periods which only came to an end in 1798 and 1844, so obviously the book could not be properly understood before those dates. This would seem to indicate that the time of the end - the period of time immediately preceding the Second Coming - began about the middle of the nineteenth century.

In the time of the end many will travel widely to increase knowledge, or if we accept the more traditional translation, many will travel widely and knowledge will be increased. In either case we have an accurate description of our modern world. Never before have so many people travelled so widely, by land, sea and air. Never before has so much been known about the world and the universe.

This century has seen an unprecedented explosion in both travel and knowledge. Literally millions of people travel to foreign lands for business or for their holidays. Human beings have travelled at incredible speeds, circling the earth in a mere ninety minutes and voyaging as far as the moon. This, and the amazing inventions that surround us in our homes, confirms that we are living in the time of the end.

" 'Then I Daniel looked, and there before me stood two others, one on this bank of the river and one on the opposite bank. One of them said to the man clothed in linen, who was above the waters of the river, "How long will it be before these astonishing things are fulfilled?" '

" 'The man clothed in linen, who was above the waters of the river, lifted his right hand and his left hand towards heaven and I heard him swear by Him Who lives for ever, saying "It will be for a time, times and half a time." When the power of the holy people has been finally broken all these things will be completed.' " Daniel 12:5-7

No doubt this question refers to the events described in chapter eleven, these are the "astonishing things" about which the anonymous questioner enquires. With a gesture that finds its echo in the book of Revelation, the heavenly being who has been conversing with Daniel swears by God that time will last for three and a half years.[3] Because exactly the same words are used as in Daniel chapter 7, we may be confident that the same time period is intended, the period of 1,260 years between 538 AD and 1798 AD.

This is the second time that the book of Daniel has referred to the destruction of the "holy people"[4] which Daniel himself would have understood as a reference to the Jews. In view of the turbulent events in Palestine brought to view by chapter 11 it is interesting to speculate that perhaps Israel will not always win its battles with the Arabs. In that case we may expect the end to come soon after Israel is destroyed. This, of course, is speculation and no doubt other interpretations are possible.

"'I heard but I did not understand. So I asked, "My lord, what will the outcome of all this be?' He replied, "Go your way, Daniel, because the words are closed up and sealed until the time of the end. Many will be purified, made spotless and refined but the wicked will continue to be wicked. None of the wicked will understand, but those who are wise will understand. From the time that the daily sacrifice is abolished and the abomination that causes desolation is set up, there will be 1,290 days. Blessed is the one who waits for and reaches the end of the 1,335 days. As for you, go your way till the end. You will rest and then at the end of the days you will rise to receive your allotted inheritance."'" Daniel 12:8-13*

Various suggestions have been made concerning these two time periods. In view of the fact that they are so similar in length to the 1,260 days many regard them as extensions to the 1,260 days, added on to either the beginning or the end. The problem is that we are given no identifying marks for either the beginning or the ending of these periods, and so may do with them as we please.

The catch, of course, lies in the implication that it is the wicked who will not be able to understand them. Every expositor has therefore felt obliged to defend his probity by "explaining" these time periods. It is obvious, however, that Daniel was not to understand these periods of time but was to rest until the end when he would be resurrected. As Daniel was not lacking in spiritual insight we may therefore conclude that there was a second factor involved in understanding them, namely, that when the time is ripe they will be understood.

I have not yet come across an interpretation that is truly satisfactory, nor have I been able to think one up for myself. I therefore leave this as one of the mysteries of God which will, in due time, be made plain to His children. For myself I am content, if that is the will of God, to rest confident that, through the merits of Jesus my Lord, I will receive my inheritance at the end of days.

It is my earnest prayer that you who have read so far may have the same hope, and that this little work will have helped you in some measure to a better understanding of God's will. To Him be all glory and honour.

---

1. Traditionally Michael is regarded as one of the four archangels, Gabriel, Azariah and Raphael being the other three. Gabriel is mentioned in Daniel and in Luke and is identified as the

angel who stands in God's presence. The other two are only mentioned in the apocrypha and probably owe more to Jewish folk-lore than Divine inspiration.

Michael, who is mentioned in the books of Daniel and Jude, is no-where called an angel but "one of the chief princes" and "the great prince". When Michael arises the dead are resurrected, an event which we know will take place at the Second Coming of Jesus, so it is at least likely that Michael and Jesus may be identical, a suggestion that may be strengthened by the fact that the name Michael means "Like God" in Hebrew.

We can be sure of this, however. If Michael is the heavenly name for Jesus then Michael is not an angel but the Son of God.

2. For example, Zechariah 13:8 - 14:2 speaks of two thirds of those who profess to be God's people being killed amid scenes of violence. It is not enough to have an outward appearance of being right with God. We must make sure that, to the best of our ability, we have confessed and forsaken every sin and that we are living up to all we know of God's will. We must make sure that Jesus is truly our Lord and that nothing He asks us to do has been neglected.

3. Revelation chapter 10 shows us the same being standing on the sea and on the land, raising his hand and taking the same oath to declare that "There will be no more delay." (Or as the King James version has it, "There shall be time no longer.") Doubtless the messenger of Revelation 10 is referring to the period predicted in Daniel.

However in both Daniel and Revelation, the end of prophetic time does not mean the end of time. Revelation says that the end comes after the seventh trumpet has sounded, Daniel says that it will come when the holy people (the Jews) have been finally "broken".

It follows that Revelation chapter 11 should be of particular interest to us as it describes events between the end of the 1,260 years - that is, events after 1798 AD - and the end of time. Needless to say, that particular chapter of Revelation is extremely difficult to interpret, probably because we are living in the middle of it!

4. Daniel 8:24 is the other reference.

Index